D1600855

My Exit Plan

Getting My House in Order

RHONDA D. GREEN

ENDORSED BY PASTOR JOHN K. JENKINS, SR.

Copyright

Disclaimer

This book is designed to provide information to our readers. It is sold with the understanding that the publisher is not engaged to render any type of psychological, legal, or other kind of professional advice. The content of each article is the sole expression and opinion of its author. No warranties or guarantees are expressed or implied by the publisher's choice to include any of the content in this volume. Neither the publisher nor the individual author(s) shall be liable for any physical, psychological, emotional, financial, or commercial damages, including, but not limited to, special, incidental, consequential, or other damages. Our views and rights are the same: You are responsible for your own choices, actions, and results. Some names and identifying details have been changed to protect the privacy of individuals.

Endorsement

My Exit Plan by author Rhonda Green gives a comprehensive, step-by-step approach to handling end-of-life matters based on her personal experiences and years of expertise as funeral manager for the First Baptist Church of Glenarden, Maryland. It is a much-needed guide for both individuals and churches, given the fact that everyone will experience death at some point in their lives. The information contained in this book has been beneficial to me and my family on a personal level in caring for both of my parents. I have seen many others benefit as well from the knowledge presented in this text. I have also witnessed the devastation experienced by families who are not prepared for death or its impact.

This book will offer peace of mind and much-needed preparation for the inevitable transition from this life, while presenting the necessary processes and procedures for end-of-life planning.

John K. Jenkins, Sr.

Senior Pastor

First Baptist Church of Glenarden

Dedications to the Memory of

My father, Lawrence Jackson, who taught me at the age of five to cherish memories, and my mother, Doris O. Payne Jackson, for seeing God's gift in me at the age of four.

My godparents, Joseph and Pauline Fraser, for fulfilling their role as parents after my mom passed.

Chairman of the Deacon's Ministry at First Baptist Church of Glenarden (FBCG), Elder Frank Grier, for knocking on my door repeatedly for several years to complete and update his Exit Plan.

My mentor, Lula M. Jenkins, Owner of JB Jenkins Funeral Homes, Inc., for pouring into my life and teaching me the ABCs and 123s of funeral services.

My Proverbs 31 Woman, Mother Lucy V. Jenkins, for sharing her pearls of wisdom and encouraging me to walk this journey even when the road got rough, and my buddy, John J. Jenkins, for teaching me to slow down.

Former marketing director at FBCG, Iris Skinner, for inspiring me to put this book together.

My God-given brother and his wife, Timothy and Janis Boyette, who desired to have their house in order and allowed me to sit with them as they completed their Exit Plan.

My supporter, Joann Kent, a gatekeeper on my job and a very dear friend who verbally completed her Exit Plan and made sure I understood what she wanted. Prior to her transition, she requested copies of the Exit Plan to share with other employees and visitors.

PRECIOUS MEMORIES

OF THE PEOPLE

THAT HELPED TO SHAPE AND MOLD ME

Acknowledgements

I thank God for granting me the gift of compassion to serve others.

A special thank you to my husband, Ron; my daughter, Shallon; my adopted daughter and niece, Holly; and my grandchildren, Robert (Sean), Dashauna (DaDa), Nadja, Amari, and Little Charles for caring for my disabled son, Dialo, thereby allowing me to spend countless hours serving other families.

To my mother-in-love, GG; my bonus sons, Warees Karriem and Bernard Gibson (wife, Tanesia); my brother, Lawrence Jackson (wife, Vernadine); my sister, Minister Diane Williams; my in-laws, Doris Green, Tyrone Green (wife, Addaway), Bennie Green (wife, Ruth), and Teresa Green-Moses, thank you for loving me unconditionally and understanding my work schedule.

To my shepherd, Pastor John K. Jenkins, Sr., Senior Pastor of the First Baptist Church of Glenarden, thank you for entrusting your members to my care.

To my supervisor, First Lady Trina Jenkins, thank you for believing in me to do what God has gifted me to do.

To my former supervisor, Stacey Fleming, Director of the Events Department at FBCG, thank you for allowing me to spread my wings and fly with my God-given gift (while on the job).

To my God-given mother, Sophia Boyette; sisters, Geneva Pearson, Gwendolyn Scott, Reverend Shirley Dawson, Nicole Graves, Jacqueline Harrison, Marie Saint Aubin, Melody Boyette Hendrick, and Janel Kennedy; my dear friend, Ilean Mathias; my nieces, Charita Matthews, Sandy Saint Aubin and Taimiko Jackson Hayes (husband, Nic); and my nephew, Christopher Pearson, for helping me put my thoughts into words, encouraging me along the way, spending countless hours editing and working on numerous logos and website designs.

To Gwendolyn Hicks, thank you for assisting me in the FBCG Funeral Services Department as the Funeral Coordinator, and I also thank you for your continued support with *My Exit Plan.*

To Gregory Duckett, Glenda Freeman and Daniel Payne, thank you for your willingness to share your years of experiences and knowledge, and for allowing me to shadow you in the funeral industry.

To Etan and Nichole Thomas, Dr. Celeste Owens, Fred Johnson, Reverend Belynda Gentry, Faye Burnette, Angela Hendrix Bell, Nelson Anderson and Chris Saulter (Minuteman Press), Wanda Milian and Mary Jones, thank you for your contributions to this project.

And to the Honorable Cereta A. Lee, Register of Wills for Prince George's County, Maryland, thank you for your wisdom, guidance, and support to the people I serve.

Table of Contents

ENDORSEMENT i

DEDICATIONS TO THE MEMORY OF ii

ACKNOWLEDGEMENTS v

INTRODUCTION 1

CHAPTER ONE: HOW IT ALL GOT STARTED

My Story 3
Taking My Own Advice 6

CHAPTER TWO: GETTING MY HOUSE IN ORDER

My Exit Plan 9
What Is an Exit Plan? 9
Why Is It Difficult for Some People to Create a Plan? 10
Other Documents Needed with an Exit Plan 11

CHAPTER THREE: EVERY FAMILY HAS A DIFFERENT EXPERIENCE

A Family without a Plan 13
    The Single Professor without a Plan 14
    Grandma's Hands 16
    What Goes Around Comes Around 18
    They Almost Turned the Casket Over 19
    Who is the Beneficiary? 20
    I'm Your Brother 21
    I want that Flag! 23
    My Dad's Guns 24
    This Can't Be True 25
    After Thirty Years of Marriage 26
    Looking Out for My Best Friend 27

The Family That Is Represented by the Government, State, or an Organization 29
    My White House Experience 29
    A Fallen Officer 33

A Family with a Plan 36
    Living a Good Life with Downs Syndrome 36
    My Family Experiences 37

CHAPTER FOUR: DEATH WITHOUT AN EXIT PLAN

Minor Setbacks 45
Division in the Family 46
Loss of Benefits 47
Loss of Property 47
Lack of Closure 48

CHAPTER FIVE: THE BENEFITS OF AN EXIT PLAN

To Keep Your Family with One Accord 49
Proper Distribution of Assets 49
Time for Closure 49
Now that I've Told You, Let Me Show You 50

CHAPTER SIX: MAKING ARRANGEMENTS

Pre-arrangements 55
Life Insurance 55
Insurance for Infants & Children up to Ages Twenty-Six 56
Insurance for Adult Children Ages Twenty-Six and Older ... 56
Repatriation Insurance 56
A Portrait of A Friend 59
Selecting a Funeral Home 60
Service Preferences 61

CHAPTER SEVEN: PRODUCTS & SERVICES

Standard Caskets 63
Oversized Caskets 63
Transportation 63
Out-of-State Burials 64
Choosing a Cemetery 64
Casket Liners and Vaults 64
Headstones and Memorials 64

CHAPTER EIGHT: DISPOSITION OF REMAINS

Burial Preferences 65
Cremations 65
Organ Donation 66
Whole Body Donation 66

CHAPTER NINE: WHAT IS NEEDED TO COMPLETE A SERVICE

Death Certificates 67
Programs 68
Service Participants 68
What Your Family Should Know 68
Obituaries 68
Policies of the Church and Other Venues 69
Policies for Funeral Homes 70

CHAPTER TEN: FILING FOR BENEFITS

Office of Personnel Management 71
Social Security 75
Veterans Affairs 78
    When a Military Service Member or Retiree Dies 78
    Burial Benefits 79
    Pensions 81

CHAPTER ELEVEN: WHEN DEATH OCCURS AT HOME

When Hospice is Involved 83
When Hospice Is Not Involved 83
Home Removals 84

CHAPTER TWELVE: WHAT WE USED TO DO & WHAT WE DO NOW

Funerals Then versus Now 85
Where We Are Now – Moving Forward 85
Opening An Estate 85

CHAPTER THIRTEEN: TESTIMONIALS

A Blessing to Our Family 87
A Gift That Keeps on Giving 88
An Exit Plan Blessing 89
It All Happened So Fast 90
A Job Well Done 91
You Carried My Burden 92
A Dad with a Plan 93
Unexpected Tragedy with No Plan in Sight 94
From the Heart of a Wife 95
We Believe in Having an Exit Plan 96

CHAPTER FOURTEEN: NUGGETS FOR FUNERAL COORDINATORS

How to Effectively Plan and Coordinate a Funeral or Memorial.................... 97
Self Care 101
    How to Avoid Burnout.. 102

CHAPTER FIFTEEN: GRIEF AND BEREAVEMENT

Dealing with Grief.. 105
Grief Support 106
Knowing What to Say and What Not to Say.. 108

CHAPTER SIXTEEN: RESOURCES

Government Agencies.. 110
Grief Support Groups... 110
*The Healing Transitions and Bereavement Ministry of First Baptist Church of
    Glenarden* 110
Books on Grief and Bereavement 110
Estate Definitions 111

FROM THE AUTHOR 116

My Exit Plan

Getting My House in Order

Introduction

My sister, Diane, told me some time ago that as a young child I attended every family funeral with my mom. She reminded me that I took special interest in all the details. Mom would stop to talk to someone at the viewing, and I would slip away to pass out funeral programs and tissues and console the bereaved. These encounters stuck with me for years, and I now realize that even as a child I had been gifted with a compassionate spirit to console grieving hearts.

One day when I was twelve years old, my mom was in the kitchen cooking and received a phone call that my grandmother was very ill. I ran out and flagged down a taxicab. Mom came out and jumped in the cab, not knowing that I was in the front seat ready to go! A strange feeling had swept over me that my grandmother was dying and that I needed to be there to handle things.

When the cab stopped at 16th and U Streets NW in Washington, DC, at my Uncle Earl and Aunt Gladys' apartment, I jumped out and ran inside. As I approached the bed, my grandmother held her hand out. I grabbed it because I could see she was slipping away, and I didn't want her to go alone. Sounds a little crazy, but that began my ministry to help people transition.

Helping to plan funerals for family and friends over the years has taught me many *dos* and *don'ts*. I have come to understand that funerals and memorial services should be planned with as much care and attention to detail as the most upscale wedding or other special life event.

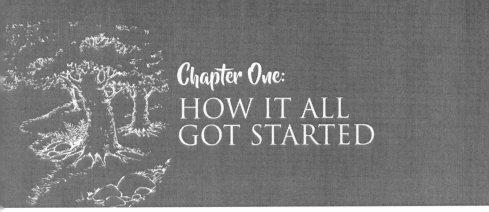

MY STORY

My first husband, Butch, became terminally ill in the early 1980s. His hospice nurse, Geneva Pearson, would come and check on him daily. On the day he transitioned, it seemed like the funeral home took forever to arrive. As the van pulled up, my brother, Lawrence, noticed there was only one person coming to the door. The man from the funeral home told us he had to wait forty-five minutes for another attendant. I must tell you that my brother, up to that point, would never have anything to do with sickness, death, and dying; he did not like hospitals or funerals. But to my surprise, he assisted the attendant with the removal of my husband's body. He stood by my side the entire time.

At that time in my life, I did not have an exit plan, I didn't know anything about selecting a funeral home, and I didn't know that veterans could be buried at a veterans cemetery for free. I spent way too much money for the service and burial, and it took forever to get benefits for my children from Veterans Affairs, the Office of Personnel Management, and from the Social Security office. It was not because those organizations did not send the check but because I did not have anyone guiding me through the process. I learned so much from this experience and made sure I was fully prepared moving forward.

In the early 1990s, my mom's health declined. Prior to her passing, I made sure we had an exit plan for when God called her home. This plan included notes from conversations with her about her desires, a power of attorney, living will, and her last will and testament. When mom passed in 1993, I thought I had it all together and that planning her service would be a walk in the park. However, there were key pieces to her plan that I had not included, like what the funeral protocol was at the church she attended and who would participate in the program. I didn't have a clue where to start, nor did I know what to ask for or what to expect from her church. I also did not have a funeral coordinator to work with or guide me through the ordeal.

Thanks to my spiritual father, Earl McJett, preparing the funeral program was a no-brainer; however, there were hundreds of other details to manage. I whined to my pastor, Rev. John K. Jenkins, about not knowing what to do and how no one was helping me. That's when the ball began to roll. Deaconess Joan Austin and others from my church provided the critical direction I needed, resulting in a wonderful homegoing celebration for my mom.

During that time, I was an Outreach Coordinator at the Suicide Prevention Center in Lanham, Maryland. I was trained to assist others during stressful times and to diffuse chaotic and difficult situations. Family members and close friends who were terminally ill would ask to come to my house to transition because they did not want to be alone. I humbly granted their wishes, as that fell in line with my passion to provide comfort and support to those who are grieving and transitioning.

In the mid-1990s, I went to work part-time as a front-desk receptionist at FBCG. Armed with the same compassion exhibited during my childhood, I always seemed to be in the right place at the right time to comfort people who were grieving. I clearly remember one afternoon when a member called the church to say that the hospital advised her to call her church for assistance because her husband was dying. Unfortunately, the caller did not like the response she received, so she came to the church to speak to our pastor. As he assured her that someone would assist her, I happened to walk by with no one else in sight. *Right place. Right time.* You guessed it! Pastor Jenkins asked me to assist her. My first thought was, *I don't know a thing about funerals!* My second thought was, *Pastor Jenkins just helped me through my mom's funeral; surely I can help this lady through her husband's.* That was the beginning of my life as the Funeral Services Coordinator at FBCG.

It took a few years for me to understand what God was doing and to grasp His vision for me. In the early 2000s, however, I saw a glimpse of His plan. God began to plant mentors in my life to groom me into mastering the ABCs and 123s of funeral services.

In 2009, the church moved my position of Funeral Services Coordinator from the Ministry Support Department to the Events Department. I didn't know how that would work out, but I knew it was a God move! In our first meeting, my new supervisor said, "You do your job, we won't have any problems. You don't do your job, we will have a problem!" I didn't know what to think, but I relied on God! I was blessed because my supervisor allowed me to spread my wings. I shared my ideas with her, and she enthusiastically responded, "Go for it!"

Within a short period of time, God opened doors for me to speak at several venues on the topics of "Taking Funerals to Another Level" and "Preparing for Your Departure."

Pastor Keith Battle asked me to speak at a Bible study at Zion Church shortly after he preached an exit plan message based on II Kings 20:1, titled "Getting Your House in Order." With his permission, I titled my first written publication *My Exit Plan*, referencing the same scripture. Over the next few years, opportunities to speak increased as I shared my passion with audiences and encouraged each of them to "get your house in order."

Since each employee on my job is tasked to set and accomplish annual goals, my goal in 2012 was to present *My Exit Plan* at our monthly staff meeting. We all know that people do not want to talk about death and dying, so I determined to add a little pizzazz by writing a funny script and drafting coworkers to perform in front of our audience.

The skit engaged the staff from the first word to the last. I had printed 400 copies of *My Exit Plan*, and they did not go to waste! One attendee told me he had never thought about life insurance, and after the meeting, he immediately took out a policy to ensure that his family had enough to cover his funeral and burial expenses. That's when I realized people were catching on and *My Exit Plan* had been birthed!

In 2013, I was offered a promotion to be the Senior Pastor's Executive Assistant. Now, let me be honest. I wanted to say NO right away!!! I thought the responsibilities would take me away from what I loved and where God had placed me. Supporting families had become my full-time passion. I loved my job and the people I served, but little did I know, God was just taking His plan to another level; in addition to becoming the Executive Assistant, I became the Funeral Services Manager. Wow! A promotion and I remained active in what God had gifted me to do.

Employees are encouraged to groom someone as their successor. Over the years, Gwendolyn Hicks had walked alongside me with funerals, and I knew beyond a shadow of a doubt that she would be the person to take my place. Because she did a phenomenal job with very little supervision, I was able to continue to help families at my church as well as other churches and organizations complete their Exit Plan.

In 2017, with an increasing load of funeral and memorial services, I asked my pastor if I could return full-time to my first passion—funeral services. He said yes. There was someone already groomed, ready, and available to assume my Executive Assistant position. I left him in good hands, of course!

As funeral and memorial activities increased, I realized the workload required the attention and care of a larger team. We were blessed with three volunteers, each with specific specialties: Ida Williams (programs and administration), Nadine Cid (administration) and Chrystal Tibbs (logistics). Each serves the Funeral Services Department with unwavering commitment, and I thank God for them.

TAKING MY OWN ADVICE

I have a disabled son who was born after twenty-five weeks of pregnancy. The doctors said repeatedly that Dialo would not make it through the day of his birth. After they placed him on life support, I decided that if he survived, it would be God's doing. He remained in the hospital for approximately six months. Upon his discharge, I was told he would not make it through his first year. Later, one year became the first five years, and once I was told that he would surely not make it past his seventeenth birthday. In 2019, we celebrated forty-two years of life for my son.

Because of Dialo's disability, he's not able to make decisions for himself, so I must make decisions for him.

Deciding who would care for my son if I should transition before him was one of the toughest decisions I have ever had to make. I vowed from the day he was born that if God allowed him to live, I would be the best mother to him his entire life and never place him in a nursing home or give him up for adoption.

In 2012, Dialo underwent orthopedic surgery, and after being discharged from the hospital, he came straight home. He needed someone at his bedside around the clock. Shallon and Holly, both moved back home to care for Dialo. I am so grateful to them for the countless hours they spent with him during that time.

Over the years, I've watched my husband, children, and grandchildren care for Dialo, and I've been comforted in knowing that they would do a good job to carry out my wish of keeping him at home, loving him, and providing the best care for him.

Despite knowing this, I still had to narrow Dialo's care down to naming a guardian—the one person who would be responsible for making decisions for him, keeping all his appointments, and making weekly trips to McDonalds for his fish sandwich. Determining who would be his guardian became an even harder task after my husband suffered a stroke in 2016. Prior to his stroke, he was able to lift our son and do everything for him that he could not do himself.

As I watched my children and grandchildren mature over the years, I realized that I needed to appoint two of them to carry out my wishes for Dialo. Additionally, I purchased a burial site for him and a policy to cover the cost of his services. I am the beneficiary of the policy, but I have appointed two contingents for if I predecease my son. As his legal guardian, I have completed a will for him with instructions of what to do if the designated guardians are unable to care for him. My prayer has been that he would predecease me so that I can make sure he is cared for all of his life and that my death would not cause disruption in anyone else's life. I know I am not in charge, though I have done my part of completing my son's Exit Plan. I leave the rest to God!

I share this because many families with disabled children do not have clearly written instructions for what should happen if both parents predecease their child or if the surviving parent is unable to care for their child. I know there are many factors to consider, but taking the proper measures and planning in advance is vitally important to ensure the child will not wind up as a ward of the state.

Not only did I complete a plan for my son but I also decided to make sure that my husband, children, and grandchildren had a plan. I realized that I did not want to be stressed out or running around at the last minute if any of them predeceased me.

Along with my husband's double stroke a few years ago came numerous blood clots in his brain. It was touch-and-go for a while, but by God's grace he is here today and functioning very well. Prior to his stroke, we had discussed what he would want should he die before me. He was adamant about being cremated. To that, his mom said, "Ohhhhh no!" Because of her response, he put his cremation wishes in writing so I could be sure to honor what he wanted; I didn't want his family to think that cremation was my decision for him. As for my children and grandchildren, I held the same conversation with each of them so that we as a family would know what was in the Exit Plan and where the plans were located, if needed.

MY EXIT PLAN

Since the publication of *My Exit Plan*, several people have completed their Exit Plan and are relieved to have a solid plan to leave their loved ones. As I move forward, my goal is to share *My Exit Plan* and the wealth of funeral services information I've attained through the years. From coast to coast, I will inform families of how to prepare their loved ones and spare them the stress of making emotionally-charged decisions under the pressure of time.

WHAT IS AN EXIT PLAN?

An Exit Plan is a completed document that includes final wishes and important information needed to carry out arrangements when a death occurs. It is made up of questions to be answered when you or a loved one transitions, in order to conduct services that meet the wishes of the deceased. Completing this document in advance allows the family to be at the bedside of a loved one when they transition rather than frantically running around attempting to put the many pieces together to carry out a service.

The Exit Plan includes your personal information: full name, aliases, maiden name, address, date of birth, place of birth, marital status, social security number, employment, retirement and/or disability history, military history for you and your spouse (including rank, branch, enlistment date, discharge date, type of discharge, and location of (DD 214), parents' information (mother's maiden name), and full name of spouse and social security number (if applicable). You should also keep your personal documents on file, including location of policies or policy information, power of attorney, last will and testament, birth certificate, legal documents, bank accounts, and attorney's information, if you have one. Make a list of the people who should be notified at the time of your death. Persons you desire to have an active role in your service should also be on that list.

I have found that having information in advance about the following makes the transition significantly smoother for families: your funeral home or crematory information along with your decision as to whether or not you want (1) a service, (2) a viewing and a service, (3) direct cremation, (4) viewing and then cremation, (5) open or closed casket, (6) glasses and jewelry on or off, and so on.

Secondly, an Exit Plan is a priceless and invaluable gift that you give to yourself and your family. It's a gift that keeps on giving! Everything is presented so that you don't have to be stressed about the next step. Once you take care of the business of dying, you can then take care of the business of living. In many cases, people have never done this before, so in addition to sharing your wishes and desires with your family, you are also teaching them how to do the same.

WHY IS IT DIFFICULT FOR SOME PEOPLE TO CREATE A PLAN?

People often ask me when is the right time to get one's house in order, and I tell them there is no right time. You just have to get it done. I find that waiting until a person is on their deathbed or when they have just received a negative health diagnosis, makes it more difficult, but if that is the only time to get it done, then do it!

It's emotionally difficult for me to visit people who are terminally ill, but as much as it bothers me, I am often at hospitals doing just that—visiting people who have decided weeks or days before their death that they want to get their affairs in order. Because of my compassion for people, I am very selective of my conversation when interviewing people who are near death. I encourage them to finalize their arrangements and once completed, they can then focus on living.

Some people just don't want to talk about death. They think that if they talk about it, sudden death will come upon them, especially if they are ill at the time. Others feel that such a conversation is not important and want to put it off until a better time; they don't understand the drama that they leave behind when they do not have a plan. In the past few years, several celebrities died without a will or a plan, leaving their families in turmoil. Given their large estates, I can't understand for the life of me why they would leave behind a legacy of confusion, causing family members to fight one another over money.

OTHER DOCUMENTS NEEDED WITH AN EXIT PLAN

Document	Purpose
Last Will and Testament, Trust and/or Pour-over Will	Reveals who you choose to be your beneficiary or trustee, to whom you will leave your earthly possessions, who will handle your business and carry out your wishes, who will care for your minor children, and many other details.
Durable/General Power of Attorney	Identifies who will act on your behalf to cover banking and other legal matters that require your signature.
Medical Power of Attorney	Allows your designated person to make medical decisions for you when you are ill and unable to make decisions for yourself.
Advanced Directive/Medical Living Will	Reveals whether you wish to be on life support, artificially fed, an organ donor, or to donate your body for scientific purposes.
Military Discharge Papers	Having a DD 214, or selected discharge papers, allows the family to complete arrangements for a military burial and will also assist in obtaining any military benefits for which the family may be eligible.
Marriage License and/or Divorce Degree	A marriage license verifies the legitimacy of a marriage. A divorce degree verifies the marriage has been dissolved.
Obituary	Details your life story along with the names of your family and friends you would like to mention; lists pallbearers and floral bearers.
Draft Order of Service	Includes the names of persons you want to speak, read, eulogize, and sing at the service.
Photos	Update the photo that will be used on the front of your program every five years, and have a selection of photos that represent the legacy of your life.
Banking Documents	Having a POD (paid on death) beneficiary on a bank account is extremely important. This frees your money so that your beneficiaries can have access to cover immediate expenses. Otherwise, your funds will be tied up in probate.
Online Account Login Information	Keep an updated list of current login information such as usernames, passwords, pins and security questions. Store this information in a secure place and indicate the location in your final documents.

Chapter Three:
EVERY FAMILY HAS A DIFFERENT EXPERIENCE

A FAMILY WITHOUT A PLAN

It is so sad when someone transitions, and arrangements are not made because the family doesn't know what to do, there is no insurance, or the next of kin does not come forward in a timely manner.

When a family has never experienced death and it happens, they can become totally numb to what the next steps should be. If they don't have a close advisor, they often sit for a few days wondering what needs to be done. Such a family would really be in bad shape if, in addition to not knowing what to do, they have no life insurance or funds to pay for the service.

I've had cases where there was no insurance and the deceased has remained at the funeral home for almost two months, and arrangements were still yet another month away. Families are often determined to have a full service with a burial, and until they can raise all the money, they wait. There are other cases where families have not had the money to carry out the services and have raised funds through internet platforms. I am not personally in favor of this, but when there are multiple deaths at the same time in the same family, I can understand using internet platforms for raising funds.

There are other instances where the deceased may have been separated from their spouse, with no communication between the two. But when death occurs, it is almost like they never separated, because the spouse is still the spouse and gets to call the shots if there is not a written document that clearly states otherwise. Take, for instance, a husband and wife who are separated and not on good terms, and the wife dies. Say the wife had children prior to her marriage to the estranged husband, and her children arrange her service. When the estranged husband shows up, everything comes to a screeching halt! Why? He is her next of kin, according to the law. Depending on the husband's heart, mom could be cremated or buried in another state (away from her children).

This is a good time to decide on "getting your house in order" to make sure this does not happen to you. For the record, I pray that from the day of birth, everyone gets an insurance policy.

The Single Professor without a Plan

Troy Anthony Jones was born in October 1969 to Charles and Mary Jones. Two days after his birth, a team of doctors met with his parents and grandmother to informed them that he was born with congenital heart disease and would probably only survive for about two weeks. However, his grandmother, with her amazing faith, boldly spoke up and said she was putting Troy in God's hands to keep him here to do great things. He was released from the hospital but faced other challenges.

When Troy turned nine, the team of doctors met with the family again, stating that Troy would need to have open-heart surgery. If they didn't do the surgery, he would not survive another year; however, there was no guarantee the surgery would be successful. The day of the surgery, the family prayed to God for Troy, and he not only survived but also thrived and experienced many accomplishments.

Because of his heart challenges, Troy's slower educational and motor development skills often hindered him in school. However, his parents continued to honor his grandmother's request to ensure that Troy was given opportunities to succeed. Although the school system provided some support, his parents enrolled him in several mainstream programs at Prince George's Community College to develop his educational and motor development skills. As a senior at Eleanor Roosevelt High School, and with encouragement by his sister, Lisa, Troy applied and was accepted by Franklin Pierce College in Rindge, New Hampshire.

In his second year of college, Troy studied abroad for a semester at Regent's College in London, England. He graduated two years later with a Bachelor of Arts degree in English. He then pursued a master's degree in elementary education at the University of South Florida. After graduating, he landed a job with Incarnation Catholic School, where he taught fifth grade for five years. He had such a unique teaching style that parents would request their child be placed in his class.

Later, Troy's former professor from Virginia Tech encouraged him to pursue his PhD at Virginia Polytechnic Institute and State University. After graduating from Virginia Tech, Troy took a job with East Carolina University in Greenville, North Carolina. Then he accepted an assistant professor position at SUNY Empire State College in New York, where he was later promoted to associate professorship with tenure.

On Thursday, November 1, 2018, I received a call that after a fruitful life, forty-nine-year-old Troy had passed away unexpectedly in New York. He died at home with no will and no beneficiary designated on his job or on his insurance policies.

That night, I contacted the New York medical examiner to arrange to have Troy identified and picked up by a New York funeral home the following day. I then contacted the New York police department to ensure his home was secured. I also contacted a probate attorney to set up his estate and a real estate agent to sell his property. Within a few hours, I was able to give his family a checklist of instructions for what to do upon their arrival in New York.

Friday morning, Mrs. Jones and Lisa drove to New York, met with the medical examiner, Troy's coworkers, and later, the funeral home. Prior to their arrival, I spoke with the funeral director to finalize the contract, and I shared the cost with the family. At that point, all I could think about was Mrs. Jones finishing her business in New York and returning home. After their meeting, the funeral home directed them to a nearby hotel, where they stayed overnight with a plan to return home that morning and then back to New York on Tuesday to pick up the death certificates. Normally it takes a few days and sometimes more than a week to get death certificates, but in this case, the funeral director surprisingly had the death certificates delivered to the hotel early on Saturday morning, two days after Troy's death.

The next step was to have Troy picked up by a Maryland funeral home in order to transport him to Maryland, where a wonderful homegoing celebration was held with his family, church members, and coworkers from New York. The service was livestreamed so that the colleges in various states where he previously attended and worked could take part in the celebration of his life.

Everyone was shocked that Troy had not designated a beneficiary. One would think that a person with his credentials would have his affairs in order. He did not, and his parents had to cover the cost of his funeral, burial, legal fees, and many other expenses. They were eventually reimbursed, but the rest of the funds will have to be processed through probate, which can take up to a year. If he'd had a will and designated beneficiaries on his insurance policy and bank accounts, their experience would have been a lot smoother.

Troy had great love and respect for his parents and sister, and he would never have intentionally left behind a situation that would cause them additional grief. I believe he just didn't know that he needed an Exit Plan. Understand that having your affairs in order will allow you and your family time to grieve rather than having to immediately focus on legal matters.

LESSON LEARNED

If you are the next of kin to your loved one, make sure you have a conversation with them to discuss their wishes. Be sure to confirm that beneficiaries have been designated.

Grandma's Hands

Charlie was one of four children. He was a hard worker and spent countless hours assisting his parents with their farm. To his surprise, when his father, Mr. Willie, died, he was left with the family home and several acres of land. His father knew Charlie would be the one to care for his mother and make sure she always had a home to live in.

When Charlie died in a tragic car accident, his mother, Ms. Mable, affectionately known as Grandma to her family, became concerned about the house and land. It had been discovered that the deed to the property was never changed. It had remained in Mr. Willie's name (Ms. Mable's Husband) since his death. Charlie's children assumed that everything was in their father's name. His oldest son attempted to take a home equity loan out on the property. Ms. Mable received a call from the bank the day before the funeral with questions about the loan request.

When she arrived at the funeral, her grandson, Vernon, told her that he was "the new sheriff in town." He explained to Ms. Mable that since his dad had passed, the property was now his. And not only that, he was going to fix the house up to sell it. Ms. Mable thought that she didn't hear Vernon clearly and asked him to repeat himself. Ms. Mable is an 85-year-old lady who walks with a cane and has severe arthritis in her hands. But for some reason that day, she was feeling pretty good. As Vernon approached his father's casket to view him for the last time, he continued to mumble that he was running things at the house. Ms. Mable pulled herself up out of the seat using her cane, walked over to Vernon, and with an open hand, she smacked him upside his head with all of her strength. Not one time, but several times. With each smack, she gave him instructions. Ms. Mable said, "Boy, as long as you live, don't you ever disrespect me again!" She further stated, "You ain't selling nothing around here." This went on for almost ten minutes. Vernon's aunts, uncles and siblings laughed uncontrollably and yelled out, "Grandma still got them hands." The service was delayed about thirty minutes so that everyone, including the pastor, could pull themselves together. During the sermon, the pastor chuckled a few times and said, "You better watch out for Grandma's hands." After the family returned home from the repast, Ms. Mable made it clear to her family that the house was still in her husband's name and that she was "the new sheriff in town."

Charlie's siblings were angry that their father left the property to him, and they distanced themselves from him. Unfortunately, this family, who had been very close-knit, became divided over the years. Charlie's children were disappointed when they found out they were not getting the promised share from the sale of what they thought was their dad's property. But that was short-lived. They eventually supported the house going back to their grandmother because they really didn't have a choice. I guess it was a good thing in this case that Charlie did not put the house in his name. But you can bet Grandma Mable handled her business.

LESSON LEARNED

Discuss your wishes with your spouse and all of the children. Verify the status of the home and check land records to verify whose name(s) are on the deed to the property.

What Goes Around Comes Around

Jonathan was married to Meredith for nearly twenty years, and together they raised two stepdaughters. This man divorced his wife and moved on. He was the only father that the girls had ever known, and they continued to have a beautiful relationship with him even after the divorce and his remarriage. Unfortunately, he became ill and suddenly died. His new wife, Charlotte, did not honor the relationship that he had with his two stepdaughters. She did not include the stepdaughters in his obituary, nor did she give them any of his personal belongings.

One of the daughters was a poet, and the other had a beautiful voice. They verbally agreed with their stepfather to recite a poem and sing at his funeral when the time came. The girls were not included in making the arrangements, so they called the wife to discuss their father's request. The call was never returned. On the day of the service, the girls showed up and noticed they were not included in the obituary nor on the program. Just as the last person got up to give remarks, the two sisters ran to the podium and said that they were the daughters of the deceased and that they wanted to honor his wishes by sharing at his service. The wife jumped up to take the microphone and tussled with them at the podium. The oldest daughter proceeded to recite her poem while the youngest daughter held the wife back. Then the youngest daughter grabbed the microphone from her sister and took off to the far side of the church singing her song. The preacher did not know what to do as they continued to push and shove each other. He said a few words and ended the service.

Meredith later found a copy of her ex-husband's old will which was previously done by an attorney and filed with the court naming her daughters as the beneficiary of three rental properties that he had purchased before his marriage to Charlotte. Because he never created or filed another will, the court honored the document. The second wife had to relinquish the properties to the girls. After the transfer of the property, the stepdaughters and Charlotte never spoke again.

LESSON LEARNED

Write down any details for your funeral. Share these notes with your current spouse and all family members indicated in the details. In addition, the current spouse should encourage preparation of a will after a new marriage.

They Almost Turned the Casket Over

After battling a long-term illness, a middle-aged woman passed away with her seven children at her bedside. Arrangements were to be made a few days after her death. Sixty days later, nothing had been done. Nearly three months passed before arrangements were finally made. Neighbors and friends were puzzled as to why this former government worker had not been funeralized and buried. The children shared that the delay was because they could not agree on a funeral home or what the disposition would be for their mother's remains. Finally, the service took place and much to everyone's surprise, the service went well. However, all hell broke loose at the end of the service. The agreement with the funeral home was for the woman to be cremated after the service. Another funeral home showed up to take the body to the state where she was born for another service and burial. The children must have forgotten that the room was filled with other family and friends as they began to scream at each other while shoving the casket back and forth. The authorities were called, and the matter had to go before the court. After several witnesses confirmed that the woman had never indicated that she wanted to be cremated, a decision was made for her to be buried in her hometown where she owned a plot. By the time the bill from the funeral home for the first service was paid, attorney fees for litigation on both sides, transportation to her hometown, the fee to the second funeral home for receiving her remains, along with the opening and closing of the gravesite, the family had spent over $15,000. In most states, if you already own your plot, you can complete a funeral service for less than $7,000. After all of the expenditures, the estate had a zero balance.

Years after the funeral, the family is still divided. The grandchildren of the deceased, who were once very close cousins, no longer spend weekends together or have their play dates.

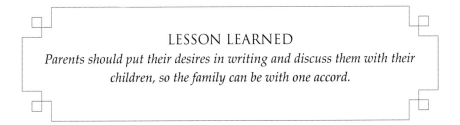

LESSON LEARNED
Parents should put their desires in writing and discuss them with their children, so the family can be with one accord.

Who is the Beneficiary?

There was nothing to worry about because this family knew that a policy for a large sum of money was in hand. The children of Cortez were able to see the monthly payment being deducted from the bank account to pay the insurance company. But they never thought to verify the beneficiaries or have a conversation with their dad about his insurance.

After the passing of this responsible man, his children went to the funeral home and cemetery to make arrangements. They chose a beautiful cherry wood casket and later selected a private mausoleum. They made all of the arrangements and notified his family and friends from as far as California. Less than a week before the service, the children submitted the insurance policy to the funeral home and the cemetery to cover the cost of the service and burial. To verify the insurance, they all signed an assignment form because they were unsure as to which of them was the actual beneficiary. Three days before the service, at the close of business, the oldest daughter received a phone call and was told that none of the children were listed as the beneficiary. They could not imagine at that point, who the beneficiary could be. The son asked his father's girlfriend of two years if she had any knowledge as to who the beneficiary was. She replied with no hesitation that they both took out large policies on each other when they met, and that the funds did not have to be used for funeral expenses. This presented a major problem because the family did not have enough cash or credit to cover the service, and the girlfriend was adamant about not paying for the service.

The service had to be rescheduled, the children had to change the casket and the burial site, and they had to come up with the cash and/or credit to pay the bills. Had they known that their dad decided to make his new girlfriend his beneficiary, they would have taken a different route from the beginning. Expecting that one of them would get at least part of the policy, his children paid several of his household bills, including the mortgage.

Most funeral homes will inform families that it takes a minimum of three business days to verify insurance. Families can make selections and arrangements before an approval. However, services are usually not rendered until the verification process is completed. If you are unsure as to who the beneficiary is, it is wise to have a backup plan. The beneficiary is not mandated to cover the cost of the funeral services.

I'm Your Brother

The mother neglected to tell her current husband and five children that she had been previously married with two children. She also neglected to tell them that she woke up one morning and walked away from her family, never looking back. The oldest son from her previous marriage was looking for an obituary in the newspaper and happened to run across his mother's name. He knew it was correct because his mother had a unique name. Her new husband and children had never met any of her family, so they decided to run the obituary in the local newspaper of the city where she was born. The son called his grandparents only to find out that they had not heard from their daughter in twenty years and had no knowledge of her whereabouts. Her parents had filed a missing person's report a few days after she disappeared. A few weeks later, the family was told by the authorities that she was okay and did not want to be found.

Her parents, siblings, and two children from the previous marriage, along with a few cousins and friends loaded up two vans and headed to their loved one's new home state to attend her funeral. The son went in first, just to make sure there was no other person with the same name as his mom. As he approached the casket, tears began to fall from his eyes, and his body weakened. He leaned on the casket and said: "Momma, why did you leave us?" The husband and son immediately embraced him, telling him that he must be in the wrong chapel. The son from the previous marriage said, "I am your brother, and this is my mother. All of my family are outside waiting to come in." They walked out, and when the current husband saw his wife's mother and sisters, he was speechless. His wife was an identical twin, and both ladies looked just like their mom. He invited them all into the service. They went to view their missing loved one, and after the service, they were able to meet with the husband and her additional children. The genes were so strong in the family that all of her children looked as though they were identical twins. There was no disputing the story, but her youngest daughter asked her daddy, "Why didn't mommy tell us about her family?"

The first set of children called their father to confirm that it was, in fact, their mother. He was traveling with his parents and siblings to the service. Shortly after that, he walked in, still not believing that this story could be true. After looking at her in the casket, he turned to the new husband and said, "I am still her legal husband."

Fortunately, because of the close resemblance of the children, they all have developed a great relationship with each other and their other family members. However, the two husbands are working through issues with her Social Security benefits and retirement from her previous employer. Because she nor her first husband had ever filed for divorce, nor did he declare her as dead, it was determined that he was legally still her husband and that her marriage to her second husband of nineteen years was not legal.

It's unfortunate that all of her children will have to live with this pain for the rest of their lives, without being able to get answers from their mother. No one will ever know why she decided to leave her family and start another one without telling them her truths.

If she wanted to move on by leaving her family, she could have at some point called or written to tell them that she was okay, but just needed to move on. This would have allowed the husband the freedom to choose a different path. The children would not have lived all of these years thinking that she was dead, since they chose not to believe the report from the authorities.

Her actions created a disastrous situation for both of her families; but more importantly, for the man that thought he was her husband.

We have to think about how the decisions we make can affect the people that we love or have once loved. Her oldest son and his sister are now very angry at her for abandoning them.

Fortunately, children under eighteen years of age and a legal husband would be eligible for Social Security benefits as well as government benefits. Unfortunately, the man that she was not legally married to would not be eligible for such benefits. He would only be entitled to an insurance policy had he been listed as a beneficiary. In some cases, the father of the minor child could receive care-givers benefits based on his income.

All of her friends in her new hometown thought that she was such a wonderful person. Both sides of the family agreed to keep their secret to themselves.

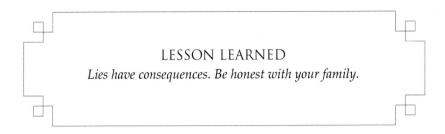

I Want That Flag!

A friend of mine passed away from multiple illnesses. His wife and two of his children preceded him in death. He had four biological children and four stepchildren. Before his illness, he had not heard from his biological children in more than twenty years. His stepchildren notified his biological children of their father's illness but never received a response. They later notified the children of his death.

In this case, the stepdaughter was the only person around to assist with medical care, appointments, and paying household bills. The father went to see his attorney and completed his will naming the stepdaughter as executor of his estate.

Funeral arrangements were made following the father's instructions left in his will. He was a veteran and received a funeral with military honors. At the end of the service, the stepdaughter who had made the arrangements received the flag, cards, and registration book. As the serviceman presented the flag to the stepdaughter, the murmurs of "that's the wrong person" began loudly. The service continued with no attention to the murmurs.

Later, there was the matter of selling two properties that were in foreclosure. The properties were sold, but there was no revenue to divide among the children. This became an ugly court battle, and there were no winners.

I applaud the stepdaughter for following the father's requests line by line. His desire was for all of his personal property and retirement to go to his sixteen-year-old daughter, who was not associated with any of his other children. At the very end, the youngest daughter received the property, and the estate was closed. The remaining children did not receive any of their father's property.

My Dad's Guns

My husband has often told me about his father being a hunter and his extensive collection of guns. He also shared that shortly after his father passed away, he and his brothers traveled back to his grandma's house where they would normally meet up to go hunting. This trip was purposely planned to collect, clean, and store the guns for future hunting trips. However, when they arrived, they noticed that the entire gun collection was no longer there. After asking others in the house, no one seemed to know where the guns had been moved. A couple of weeks later, a relative who lived close by, came forward and told them the name of the family member who took the guns.

As a young teenager who enjoyed hunting with his father and brothers, my husband was extremely devastated by the disappearance of his father's collection. He was angry for a long time at this relative, which caused a division in the family. Unfortunately, the guns were sold, and the family was not able to retrieve any of them.

This Can't Be True

About ten years ago, I shared with an engaged couple the importance of discussing their finances, insurances, and property matters. Well, they were so excited about the wedding that they never got around to having the conversation. About 300 people attended the wedding and reception, which were complete with all the bells and whistles. Everyone had a great time, including me. As I listened to them recite their vows, I wondered in the back of my mind if they had ever had the conversation. He owned a beautiful, six-bedroom home set on five acres of land with a four-car garage. The home was nicely decorated, but after the wife sold her home and moved in, she made a few changes and was happier with their home and the new in-ground pool and hot tub she had installed.

After the birth of their twins, I asked the mother if she remembered what I had suggested she and her husband talk about. She smiled and said with a little attitude, "He's a good provider for our family, and I don't have to worry about that." I knew that was my clue to step back and mind my business. But for some reason, I continued to be overwhelmed with their status of not having their affairs in order.

Suddenly, after seven years of a wonderful marriage, the husband became terminally ill and died. The wife was so devastated that she could not find the insurance policy, deed to the house, or any other important papers that would eventually be needed. She was able to withdraw enough money from the bank to pay for his funeral and burial in cash, but I received a call from her two weeks later to help her sort through his estate. When I arrived, I asked for the suitcase of papers that she had found, and to our surprise, I discovered his previous wife's name on the deed and the insurance policy and the retirement from his job. Wow!

His wife yelled out, "This can't be true! He would not have done this!"

I thought maybe it was an old deed, so we did a property search, only to confirm that the information before us was indeed correct. Not only was his previous wife the co-owner of the house, but she and their four children were also the beneficiary on both of his insurance policies. All of his children received his retirement because it was set aside for any child born to him.

Because of the way the house was titled, the previous Mrs. X more than likely will become the sole owner of the house, and she also received the life insurance. The current Mrs. X received 50 percent of what her husband had in the bank. And, by the way, there was no will or trust.

I recently spoke to Mrs. X to get permission to include her story, and we agreed to keep her anonymous. She did say that she wished she had listened and followed through with the Exit Plan discussions. To this day, it is my understanding that the estate has not been settled and that Mrs. X had to find employment in order to care for her two young children. My take on this is that had she known the house was still in her husband's and his previous wife's names, she would never have spent the money from the sale of her home for a pool and remodeling. She probably would have purchased an insurance policy leaving herself as the beneficiary. Or maybe she would not have married him if he decided he was not going to change what he had in place.

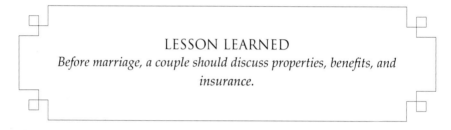

LESSON LEARNED
Before marriage, a couple should discuss properties, benefits, and insurance.

After Thirty Years of Marriage

When you marry a veteran who has been married before, make sure the two of you take a trip to the Veterans Affairs (VA) office to update the records.

A sweet little couple in their late 70s were often seen walking hand-in-hand through the mall or having a meal together. After thirty years of marriage, the husband had a stroke and died the same day. This was a tragedy for his wife. It was an even bigger tragedy when she tried to apply for his military benefits only to find out that his first wife was still listed as the spouse even though she had died ten years before he remarried. VA needed her death certificate, and the living spouse did not know any of the deceased spouse's relatives to contact. It took about eighteen months to work through this process and to present the death certificate.

She eventually received the benefits, but it was very stressful for her to know that even though she had been married to her husband for thirty years, during those eighteen months, she could not access his benefits. My heart broke for her, but all I could do was make call after call until her benefits were approved. It was a joyous day when she received her first check!

Looking Out for My Best Friend

I was recently reminded of the day my best friend's companion passed away. Just hours after his death, his children showed up to the house, asking for car keys and all of his belongings. This was long before *My Exit Plan* days, but encouraging people to have their affairs in order was a part of my DNA since childhood, so it was normal for me to be concerned at this point.

Since that day, my friend and I have had a good laugh at how I drilled her with questions: Is your name on this house? Is the car you drive in your name? Is your name on the bank account?! All I could think about was my best friend being stripped of everything that she had. At the time, which was less than an hour after her companion had transitioned, she was deeply grieving with uncontrolled tears, and she responded to every question with, "I don't know!" I asked her if she remembered signing any papers at settlement for the beautiful house they had built together. Again, she did not remember. So I jumped on the computer to search for the house, and what a relief—her name was listed. Sorting through their mail, I found that she was also on the bank account and her name was on the car that she drove. After I calmed down, I realized I had been "screaming" at her the entire time.

Thankfully, we were able to move on with the arrangements and getting her life back on track. You better believe that today my friend has a plan in place, and we will never go through that kind of stress again.

The Family That Is Represented by the Government, State, or an Organization

My White House Experience

In March 2009, I was asked to assist a family after the untimely death of a loved one. A husband and father named Smile Saint Aubin suddenly became ill, and died in the hospital. I met with his wife, Marie, and their three children to discuss the arrangements for their beloved husband and father. Since Smile had served five United States presidents during his tenure at the Blair House and the White House, I also met with Rear Admiral (R) Stephen Rochen, then Director of the Executive Residence and White House Chief Usher. To prepare for the service, Admiral Rochen visited the First Baptist Church of Glenarden. We decided that the service would be held at the smaller, more intimate location known as the Ministry Center.

Later that day, I traveled to the Saint Aubin family home in Maryland, where Sandy, their oldest daughter, graciously greeted me and quietly mentioned that one of the former presidents was on the phone offering his condolences and encouragement. Then she led me to Smile's office, where I later met with the rest of the family to work on the details for his funeral service. While in his office, which Smile had affectionately called the Blue Room, I became mesmerized with the numerous photographs of him with various presidents and several mementos of his years at the White House including Easter eggs from annual White House Easter Egg Rolls and ink pens engraved with presidents' names. In that moment, I was keenly aware that I was firmly on my destiny path.

As I sat in the well-appointed office with Sandy developing Smile's obituary, she shared that her dad was born in Haiti and came to the United States in

1973. Two years later, he met and married the love of his life, Marie, who was also born in Haiti. Sandy spoke highly of her dad. She noted that he began his career with the federal government in 1987 at the State Department. His office was located on Pennsylvania Avenue in Washington, DC, at the Blair House (officially called "The President's Guest House"), across the street from the White House. Smile had served foreign heads of states such as kings, queens, presidents from other countries, and prime ministers.

In 1991, Smile was hired to serve at the White House as a Houseman in the Executive Residence, and in 1997, he became a White House Butler, where he served with pride for nearly twelve years until his untimely death. Sandy reflected on his life: "My dad had twenty-two years of service with the federal government … he was honored to serve five United States Presidents: President Ronald Reagan at the Blair House, President George H. W. Bush, President Bill Clinton, President George W. Bush, and President Barack Obama at the White House."

When interviewing family members, I always ask about their loved ones' relationship with God. I found out that at the invitation of a friend, Marie and Sandy had attended a Sunday service at my church. They were both so moved by the message that Marie, a life-long Catholic, had joined the church. When they shared their experience with Smile, his response was, "Find me a good Baptist preacher, and I will go to that church." A few weeks later, he accompanied Marie and Sandy to church and on occasion thereafter. He soon decided that FBCG was for him too! Smile and Sandy planned to attend and join the following Sunday, not knowing that would be his last visit.

The day before Smile became ill, and while in the hospital fighting for his life, Sandy asked Pastor Jenkins' wife, First Lady Trina, to pray for her dad. Sandy wanted to make sure that her father had a relationship with God, not knowing that they would be planning his funeral a few days later.

We took a break, and I went to spend a little time with Smile's son, Rico, and youngest daughter, Stephanie. (As a counselor, I always look to engage the whole family.) Even though they both were very quiet, they spoke of their dad's outstanding character, and remembered him as a great father and a great provider. I could see that this family had never experienced death as close as this, and they were lost and grieving Smile's death. As I asked questions, they began to share and become illuminated with excitement, which created a bond between them. Immediately, I realized that Rico would step into his dad's shoes to be a support for his family. I also realized that Stephanie was Smile's baby girl and that she was already missing her dad, her hero!

The family contacted a local funeral home to handle Smile's service. Over the next few days, we continued to work on the program and made several visits to the church to discuss the details for this unique service and repast. This was a very different type of service for me, as I coordinated my efforts with White House Logistics and the Secret Service; so many pieces to this very large puzzle needed to come together. After several meetings, security checks, and conversations, we were ready to proceed with the service.

A private viewing was arranged for the immediate family at the funeral home. That morning, I sat with the owner of the funeral home in a lobby lined with photographs of President Obama. Without warning, several black trucks pulled up, and the owner excitedly asked, "What's going on?" At that moment, in walked the First Lady of the United States, Michelle Obama. Mrs. Lula Jenkins nearly fainted. She had a special love for the Obamas and could not believe Mrs. Obama was in her facility. First Lady Michelle sat gracefully while we waited for the family to arrive. After spending time with Smile's family, she briefly spoke with the owner, and they embraced like old friends. That encounter became a lifetime moment that Mrs. Jenkins would cherish forever.

I spent the rest of the afternoon briefing the church staff on the intricate details and logistics to prepare for this high-profile, yet discreet, funeral service, which was scheduled for the next day. On the morning of Smile's service, the Events and Facilities teams executed a plan to secure the parking lot to receive Secret Service staff, former presidents, dignitaries, family, and guests. Catering and Hospitality teams were ready to serve a Haitian-style dinner after the service, the details of which had been previously planned to include entrance and exit plans and seating and food-service logistics. The Pastoral and Ministry

Support teams were strategically in place to assist with greeting and escorting guests to predetermined designated areas. The Music Department was also poised to serve.

That morning, family, friends, and White House staff began to arrive right on cue for the viewing. After a two-hour viewing, Pastor Jenkins, the former presidents, and the ministerial staff processed into the sanctuary and the service began. It was beautiful. We were honored to hear from Pastor Jenkins, First Admiral (R) Rochen, President and Mrs. Bill Clinton, and former First Lady Barbara Bush, among others. Several family members were so inspired that they later joined Marie as FBCG members.

A few days later, President Obama planned a memorial service for Smile to take place at the White House. Working with Rear Admiral Rochen, I assisted with coordinating yet another service for Smile Saint Aubin. I felt like I had a traveling funeral service team when the church van pulled up to the White House gate. The service was respectful, and President Obama and First Lady Michelle spoke eloquently of Smile and the impact he had left on their family and the White House. A reception followed the service.

After Smile's death, his daughter Sandy gave birth to a beautiful baby girl, Chloe. She is the light that reminds the family that Smile lived! Chloe is growing up to be a very intelligent young lady, and she loves to spend girly time with her auntie, Stephanie.

Why do I share this story? Not everyone has a team of people to ensure that every "i" is dotted and every "t" is crossed when making funeral arrangements. Smile's death was unexpected, and his family had no idea which way to turn or what to do. But because of his tenure at the White House, all they had to do was show up. The intricate details were already planned for them.

Since Smile's death, several members of the Saint Aubin family have prepared a personalized *My Exit Plan* and are now confident that their house *will be in order* when death knocks. It is my goal to ensure that each family who requests my help receives appropriate and well-appointed funeral or memorial services that are appropriate to their loved one.

A Fallen Officer

Through the years of coordinating funerals, I have served families of several police officers, firemen, and military members. I don't recall ever having coordinated the service of a fallen officer, until Detective Jacai Colson. Learning law enforcement protocol for funeral services was a life-changing experience. I met several times with the Special Operations Division of the police department to tour the funeral location; nail down the building layout; and determine logistics that included who should enter what door, seating, parking, etc. I had recently worked with members of the Special Operations Team on a former county official's funeral, so I was at least familiar with seating and parking protocol.

After numerous meetings with county staff, I spent time engaging in heartfelt conversations with the officer's parents. I remember those conversations as though they were yesterday; the mom had walked in and hugged me as if we were old friends. I later found out that the officer's academy graduation had been held at my church and that his mom was very appreciative that he was returning to the place that had launched his career.

I understood that this man was not just another fallen law enforcement officer; he was a son and a brother. He was Mr. and Mrs. Colson's firstborn son and the big brother and protector of Jurea Colson. Jacai was born in 1987 in Philadelphia, Pennsylvania. His father had chosen the Jacuí River in Brazil as the inspiration for his name. Now it was my job to find out what their wishes were for their twenty-eight-year-old son. He loved sports, and even played football his freshman year at Randolph Macon College in 2005. Jacai graduated from the Police Academy in 2012 and became a Prince George's County patrolman. Later he became a detective on the undercover narcotics squad. He loved his work and put forth everything he could to make sure the community was safe.

Jacai's parents were very clear about what they did and did not want for their son's funeral service. As I sat and listened to them share Jacai's story, I felt like I personally knew him. Parental love radiated through the stories of his family life. Hearing how he was reared by a loving family, understanding his connection with his younger brother, and looking at literally hundreds of photos from birth to his life as Detective Colson, gave me insight on how to plan his service.

Retired Prince George's County police officer Lieutenant Chrystal Tibbs is a member of my funeral team. In Jacai's case, her knowledge of law-enforcement funeral protocol was invaluable: She knew who to call in the various county departments. She arranged my attendance at crucial meetings where logistics specific to the law-enforcement community were discussed. After several meetings that detailed building layout, entering and exiting protocol, proper formation, and seating arrangements for officers, we held a rehearsal to ensure everyone understood the order of service. Together, we orchestrated a wonderful homegoing celebration for Detective Colson that followed the customs and traditions of a service fit for a fallen hero.

On the day of the service, people arrived before the morning sunrise. The church quickly filled with thousands of family members, friends, community members, firemen and police officers from various states. The crowd overflowed into the hallways and outside.

My job did not end at the close of the service or after the thousands of guests left. Walking the family through the next steps of setting up Jacai's estate was just as important as getting through the service. Because the Colsons encouraged their sons to have their affairs in order, the family was able to conduct estate business smoothly.

"... *knowledge of law-enforcement funeral protocol was invaluable* ..."

A Family with a Plan

Living a Good Life with Downs Syndrome

Joseph Robinson, aka "Joe" was born in 1958 to Carolyn Robinson and the late Joseph Robinson Sr. During that time, the life expectancy for persons with Down syndrome was no greater than age thirty. Joe attended schools in the District of Columbia, and at the age of twenty-one, he graduated from H. Winship Wheatley Special Center in Prince George's County, Maryland, with numerous medals for participating in the Special Olympics. Over the years, he worked at Safeway, the Waffle House, the US Courts of MD, and The Gallery of Serengeti, to name a few. Joe had a heart of gold and enjoyed serving his customers.

He also loved to dance, and on any given day you could find him imitating Michael Jackson. I remember Joe attending my thirtieth wedding anniversary party at my house with his mother, Carolyn. He danced all night long to the oldies-but goodies sung by my cousin Prentiss Floyd that evening. He was the life of the party and a joy to be around. Joe traveled with his family and friends and enjoyed several cruises. He had a good life!

With all of the excitement and good times in Joe's life, because he was medically diagnosed with a condition known as Down syndrome, the state of Maryland required that he have a legal guardian to handle his affairs. His mother, being familiar with the Exit Plan for many years, knew she had to have a plan in place for Joe … and she did! Carolyn designated two of his younger siblings to care for him should something happen to her. That was just the first step. She also knew what funeral home she was going to use and where he would be buried, and she had set aside funds to cover the expenses for when that time came.

On December 6, 2016, Joe transitioned at the age of fifty-seven. His family was blessed to have him twenty-seven years beyond his life's expectancy. Because his mom had a plan, he had a beautiful service, and she and his five siblings were able to process their grief and cherish his memory.

My Family Experiences

Tracy McIntosh was a beautiful, warm-spirited young lady. I met her through my God-sister Gwendolyn Davis Scott. Gwen was best friends with Tracy's mom, Cynthia, and auntie to Cynthia's daughters, Tracy and Trina. Tracy birthed two daughters, Devin and Taryn, whom she loved and adored with all of her heart. During the birth of Taryn, she experienced extreme pain in her leg, and the doctors could not figure out what was happening. Later that day, the doctor informed us that her leg broke at the hip. Eventually we were told she had cancer and that they had to amputate her leg.

Tracy was a real trooper. Shortly after her amputation, she was discharged to her home, and it was only a matter of days before she was up and at it again. She received treatment and went into remission for several years. Tracy became a pro at using her crutches, which helped her get around as well as a person with both legs. She was a busy young lady, always helping other people, including me. One year she came to my house to decorate my Christmas tree, and I watched in amazement as she maneuvered around my seven-foot tree with one leg and a crutch.

Tracy also managed to get around with her infant daughter strapped to her chest. One day, when I went to the house to check on her, she did not answer the door or the phone. I was devastated, thinking that something had happened to her. Her neighbor told me she had left that morning with the baby and had not returned. Shortly thereafter, Tracy came stepping off the bus with the baby and shopping bags from the Hecht Company. I could not believe she had gone Christmas shopping. Well, that was her life story; she didn't let anything stop her from doing what she wanted to do.

Years went by and Tracy continued to live a wonderful life. Her cancer later returned, and we were told it had metastasized. Tracy was eventually placed in a hospice home, and I knew I had to help her get her affairs in order. After talking to her sister, Trina, I approached Tracy with a request to know her end-of-life desires. Tracy, my sweet little angel who never gave me a moment's trouble, told me she did not want to talk about dying. By this time, I had become an auntie to Tracy and Trina. So as family, I was thinking about her two daughters that she birthed and another daughter, Taylor, that God had blessed her with. I knew I had to get through to her one way or another. Trina and I both explained to Tracy the importance of making decisions and completing her will.

Finally, she agreed to having a conversation about her desires for her final arrangements and her children. We knew who would raise the three girls and what her final wishes were. From that day on, we were able to focus on her living. A few months later, Tracy transitioned, and we held a beautiful homegoing service for her. Cynthia (Tracy's mother) transitioned prior to Tracy. Tracy's girls have grown up to be beautiful young ladies, and her sister, Trina, is the owner of TMAC The Spa and is in the final stages of completing her Exit Plan.

Romell Jackson, my oldest brother, had a learning disability and as a part of my mom's Exit Plan, he came to live with me after she transitioned. My mom had a small policy on him from years ago, so I knew that the first thing I needed to do was get an insurance policy on him that would cover his funeral and burial expenses for when that time came.

Relocating from Washington, DC to Maryland was a significant change for Romell. He missed not being able to walk everywhere and speak to the neighbors as they sat on their front porches. But thank God, all the next steps fell right into place—from changing doctors, learning how to safely cross a major highway at the light to go to the store to surprise his nieces and nephews with candy, meeting new friends, including an elderly gentleman up the street whose house he often visited, and Rossie and Nicole Graves. Rossie became his best friend. They kept each other laughing.

Romell also had a great love for painting and took pride in making sure that every room in my home was painted whenever needed. And when he finished with my house, he would go and paint for our sister, Diane, and my friend, Nicole. In addition to painting, one of Romell's pastimes was telling jokes with my husband.

In 2009, Romell's doctor told him that he was terminally ill and would be transferred to a hospice facility. But, Romell just wanted to go home, so my husband and I picked him up and brought him home.

Later that day, Romell called our sister and asked her to come and pray with him. Diane was serving in the Evangelism Ministry at First Baptist Church of Glenarden under the leadership of her mentor, Rev. Shirley Dawson, and had been sharing the gospel with Romell for some time. During this particular conversation, he talked about his life and his desire to have a closer relationship with God and get baptized. My sister thought about doing it herself, but since she was not yet a licensed minister, she called an ordained minister who agreed to come out and assist with baptizing him.

Much to our dismay, Romell's health continued to decline rapidly and again, he was hospitalized. But he made it very clear that he wanted to be at home, and shortly thereafter, we honored his request and he returned home.

As we maneuvered his wheelchair into the house, he looked around and told us that we must make sure the house was painted whenever needed. Then he complimented himself, saying, "Wow! I used to paint this whole house by myself."

A month later, my sister was at the house and realized that Romell was transitioning and had not yet been baptized, so she reached out to Rev. Shirley Dawson, who was on travel at the time. Rev. Dawson told her that since time was of the essence, to just do it herself. And because she was desperate to honor his request, that girl grabbed this big old bucket, filled it with water, and baptized him as he lay in bed. And that's when he took his last breath.

When I arrived home, I could not for the life of me figure out why the floor was flooded in his room. Now, every time I picture Diane running with the bucket of water and baptizing Romell in the bed, I become consumed with laughter, and I also remember with gratitude what she did.

My point is, listen to your loved ones. Whether their last request is to take a trip, get their affairs in order, or just go out for an ice cream cone, take time to honor their wishes.

Norita Ann Austin was my oldest sister and a no-nonsense person. During my early childhood, she took me under her wing and spent countless hours with me shopping, cooking, watching movies, and visiting museums. I also spent a lot of time in her closet trying on her numerous colors of leather and suede Nineteens—a fashionable sling back shoe from the 60s and 70s, which she allowed me to wear to school.

Norita was a registered nurse, a caregiver, and my "Shero." As we got older, however, our relationship distant. But then in her senior years, we began to communicate again ... often. She would inquire about the work I do. One day when she asked what I thought about cremation, I shared that I believe it is a choice. She then asked if I would take responsibility and honor her request of wanting to be cremated. I responded, *"By all means."*

In June 2016, Norita transitioned. She had made it very clear prior to her death that she did not want a funeral. I knew what I had to do to honor her request, but I also knew that I needed closure. So I had her cremated and later hosted a memorial service and repast with a few close coworkers and friends at my house. I have such a good feeling that I did what she wanted me to do.

James Clifford (Cliff) Payne, Sr. was one of my mother's favorite nephews. She loved him so much that I thought he was a hidden secret and someday I would find out he was really my brother. Well, I was wrong. I found out that he was her favorite because she cared for him during her young-adult years.

Cliff met and married the love of his life, Ella Louise. Together, God blessed them with six children and later, a house filled with grand- and great-grandchildren. Along with his wife, he was one of the founders of a church in Upper Marlboro, Maryland. They engaged their children in ministry with them as they spearheaded Innervision Puppet Production.

They also owned James Television Hotel Service for over fifty years, which Cliff operated with his sons, Tony (James, Jr.), Louis, and Keith.

Cliff was unique. He had a lot of childhood challenges that, unfortunately, he took to his grave. You had to know him to understand him. As an adult, he opened his home to everyone. As he sought love and affection, he would give his last dime to anyone in need. In his later years, he took special interest in his brothers, Ernest and Prentiss. Cliff often traveled to the nursing home where Ernest resided, lugging his musical equipment to provide entertainment for the residents. On weekends, he ventured out to support Prentiss at his oldies-but-goodies singing engagements. This was his way of lovingly supporting his brothers.

Known as the Grill Master, Cliff could be found any afternoon preparing dinner on his six-burner grill that sat on his extra-large, multi-level deck built for family. He would often call while cooking and say, "Just come by!" When I arrived, he would prepare for me a hefty plate with my favorite twelve-inch hotdog that I could not find any place else, and then pile on Louise's homemade side dishes. Any afternoon was like Sunday dinner. My sister, Diane, would also come by just to have an ice-cream-eating contest to see who had found the best flavor. We were ice cream lovers beyond measure; tasting a myriad of flavors, our love for one another reached through our love for ice cream.

As I matured, my relationship with Cliff developed into a sister-brother kinship. After my mother's death, Diane and I both became very close to Cliff and his family; we wanted to honor the memory of his relationship with our mother. Occasionally, I would talk about death and dying with Cliff and Louise, and he would say, "I don't want anyone looking down on me!" or "Don't put no dirt over me." As a crisis counselor, I developed very good listening skills and would try to dive a little deeper to gain a clear understanding of his comments. We all understood that when Cliff died, he did not want a viewing or service. He just wanted his immediate family to gather for a special dinner in his honor.

Several years later, Cliff began to have challenges with his health, and Diane and I would pray with him and Louise. As his health declined, Louise shared with us that their daughter Pat was also ill.

On April 11, 2014, I was sitting at my desk at work when the Lord prompted me to call Cliff's oldest daughter, Denise. Almost immediately she asked, "Did mom call you?" I told her no, I was just checking in. "Dad just passed five minutes ago!" she said.

I was shocked. We had expected Cliff to be discharged that afternoon to go home. I guess we just didn't know *which* home.

After hearing the news, my sister and I went to the house for a family meeting. We agreed that everyone would honor Cliff's request and instead of a service, the family planned a dinner.

Shortly after Cliff's death, I received a call from Beverly, (Cliff's youngest daughter), stating that Pat (his second daughter), wanted to "get her house in order." I immediately went to her house to complete her copy of *My Exit Plan*.

A few days later, Louise was taken to the hospital's emergency room. She summoned for me and my sister Diane to come right away. We both left work, and as we entered Louise's hospital room, her son, Louis, was standing at her bedside waiting for our arrival. We walked into the room slowly, not knowing what to expect. Louise sat up in the bed, boldly looked in my eyes with a penetrating stare and declared, "You know what to do, Rhonda!" Her eyes were so piercing, it felt as though she could see right through me. In a very stern voice, she said, "Pray!" As I prayed, I opened my eyes and saw she was looking directly at me. The room was silent and engulfed with a sweet spirit. She took me by the hand and again said, "You know what you got to do." Because of our spiritual connection, I was able to walk away with a clear

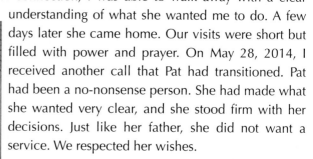

understanding of what she wanted me to do. A few days later she came home. Our visits were short but filled with power and prayer. On May 28, 2014, I received another call that Pat had transitioned. Pat had been a no-nonsense person. She had made what she wanted very clear, and she stood firm with her decisions. Just like her father, she did not want a service. We respected her wishes.

The day after Pat transitioned, Louise closed her eyes and joined her husband and daughter in their eternal resting place. Three deaths so close together in one family ... it overwhelmed me.

Talk about till death do you part! Louise and Cliff were married for fifty-five years. She was a devoted wife and mother who reared her children in the fear and admonition of the Lord, whom she dearly loved and served. She was tenderhearted, seeing only the good in people and overlooking their failures and shortcomings. No matter what difficulties she faced, Louise never complained or became disgruntled. Her character was beyond reproach, like that of a Proverbs 31 Woman.

She kept her home spotless from top to bottom and provided four-course meals for her family and anyone who visited. Her culinary specialties included corn pudding, rolls, old-fashion banana pudding, and hand-picked string beans with potatoes. And they were all *mmm* good!

As a mother, grandmother, and great-grandmother, Louise spent countless hours nurturing and praying for her family. She never missed celebrating a birthday, holiday, or graduation. Not only was she the epitome of a wife and mother, she was also a caregiver, nurse, and schoolteacher. I remember when her baby boy, Keith, was critically injured and how it seemed like it would take a miracle from God to pull him through. But Louise never gave up. She prayed night and day until he was healed.

Louise had a wonderful end-of-life celebration, and her children honored her final wishes just as they had honored her husband's and daughter's. They were able to adhere to their loved ones' requests because they had spoken with each one about what they wanted and understood what their final wishes were. This is yet another true story that I share to explain why it is so important to discuss these matters and to have a completed Exit Plan. Had this family not been engaged in conversation and prepared, this could have been a hot mess.

Shortly after Louise's death, her grandson Stefon transitioned. He was Beverly's only child, and she loved him from the depths of her heart. He left behind an unborn daughter who ended up looking like a mirror image of him. This little girl has been the heartbeat of Stefon's mom and has paved the way for her to deal with her grief.

The children of Clifford and Louise Payne have dealt with several deaths in their family. But today, aside from dealing with their grief, they are living their lives as a connected family as they continue to celebrate the memories of their loved ones. This type of connection is so needed, yet missing, in many families.

Chapter Four:
DEATH WITHOUT AN EXIT PLAN

MINOR SETBACKS

I've been amazed at how many people call their grandmother "Big Momma" and do not know her full name. It can be stressful to not know your mother's maiden name and her social security number, or your father's military discharge information. It can also be stressful when families fight over whether or not to cremate their loved one. Worse yet is the case of the grandmother who chooses to leave her insurance to her sweet little grandbabies and neglects to leave just enough to cover her funeral expenses, thus having to be cremated because there are no funds available for burial.

Other challenges include situations where the name and social security number of the deceased do not match, or life insurance policies so old that family members often don't remember that the beneficiary died forty years ago and there is no contingent. In some instances, the beneficiary was a former spouse and is now deceased, which means you must prove that someone you never met is dead.

Years ago, some families kept a lot of secrets that were usually revealed when a death occurred. Finding out, for instance, that your mother and father lived together for fifty years as husband and wife but never married because one or the other never divorced someone else ... that's shocking! Meeting sisters and/or brothers for the first time who lived a few streets over from you can be devastating. But these kinds of things happen on a daily basis.

I remember vividly a family who came into my office and dropped bundles of papers all over my desk. To pull together the pieces of paper in preparation for their loved one's service, we made several phone calls to determine who the insurance carrier was. This was a nightmare not only for the family but for me as well. In the back of my mind, I was thinking, *What in the world were they thinking ... not to have their loved one's papers in order?* After spending countless hours on the phone, we finally decided we would take care of the service first and then go back to figuring out the document disaster. That meant they had to have the cash or credit to handle the funeral home and cemetery expenses upfront. Not all families are financially positioned to cover these expenses upfront, but without the proper planning in place, one's choices become more and more limited.

In 2009, I was invited to a ladies' night out gathering. Most of the women were married, but a few were single. One young lady said she had just gotten married and wanted to know what she needed to do in order to "get her house in order." I was so glad she asked that question, because it opened the door for extended conversation. I shared with the group how important it was to know what benefits each spouse would be entitled to when one of them passed away. I also shared that having this information would aid them in knowing whether they would need to get another job or find another place to live. The bottom line is, losing one household income will likely present major changes.

In this young lady's case, she discovered that her husband's policy and retirement listed multiple beneficiaries, with the wife to receive 50 percent of a decreasing term policy. I suggested that she add her husband to her policy at work, which would give her a sure means of income should he predecease her.

A few of the ladies went home and shared the information with their husbands and the rest kept quiet. I've spoken to the young lady at least five times since we initially met. In our last meeting, I asked if she had any problems adding her husband to the policy. "I'm gonna look into it next week," she said. Her husband was diagnosed with cancer the following week. I found myself feeling angry that she had not done anything in ten years. Our last phone call ended with her telling me that she may have to give up her home.

Why do we procrastinate? It's not like the world is going to change and people are no longer going to die.

DIVISION IN THE FAMILY

Some people say that weddings and funerals can make or break a family. At a time when family members should draw closer together to support each other, often the opposite occurs. I can recall numerous occasions where families could not reach an agreement on the final funeral arrangements and everything stopped! Some family members have sat in different sections of the church for the service, and some have even attended separate repasts. Siblings can go for years after the funeral without speaking to one another.

I have encountered many situations where a person passes away and the siblings or children of the deceased want to take charge. In most states, when the deceased has a spouse, it is important to know that the spouse is considered the next of kin and by law is authorized to make the final decision in all matters. If your loved one's spouse had children prior to their marriage and the children had a relationship with the deceased, it can cause unnecessary pain if you exclude them.

When you are engulfed in chaos with your family after a loved one's death, you don't think about processing the death that has occurred. It's usually some time later that you are hit with, "My mom is gone, and no one in my family is talking to me."

LOSS OF BENEFITS

Loss of benefits can be the cause of not being able to carry out a funeral service and/or burial as planned and can also affect your ability to pay bills that are due. It can be heartbreaking when the benefits you expected to receive after the death of a loved one no longer exist. Or, not being able to find a policy that you know your loved one paid on for years can also be heartbreaking. If a policy has lapsed or the value has been withdrawn unbeknownst to you, this too can be a setback.

In 2010, my godmother died suddenly with only a partially completed Exit Plan. She left behind two paid-in-full insurance policies. To this day, we have not been able to find one of the policies, nor do we know who the insurance carrier is. This is a clear case of loss of benefits. Fortunately, because of her loving family, she had a beautiful homegoing service as planned.

LOSS OF PROPERTY

Marrying someone who divorced their spouse but never changed their beneficiary from the previous spouse to you (as the current spouse) can be a big disappointment! Oh, and let's not forget that your name is not on the deed to the house that the two of you have lived in for the past twenty years. Not only have you lost your spouse, but you could also very well lose your home or become joint tenants with the previous spouse. One thing for sure and two for certain, is that you should discuss benefits and policies before marriage and make the necessary changes on day one before you leave for the honeymoon.

Another way families lose property is by neglecting to pay the mortgage payment and not communicating with the mortgage company. And even if the mortgage is paid in full, the property taxes still need to be paid. A decision must be made as to who will pay the taxes and whether the family will refinance or sale the property. In many cases, not paying the taxes has resulted in homes being auctioned off.

LACK OF CLOSURE

Often I receive calls from families three or four days after a death to make arrangements, while their loved one is still at the hospital or morgue. The family has not contacted the funeral home because they are not sure what funds are available for a service and/or burial. In many cases, the family is at the home of the deceased, looking through papers in an attempt to figure out what they can do. Even after the service, many families without a plan cannot focus on closure because there is so much to do.

Chapter Five:
THE BENEFITS OF AN EXIT PLAN

To Keep Your Family with One Accord

After creating My Exit Plan and introducing it to families, with whom I worked. I noticed that the transition process became much smoother for family members. It was easy to get them to agree to the arrangements because their deceased loved one had either held a discussion with them or left behind clear instructions. It's awesome when a family works together to make arrangements, divide the estate, and continue with an even closer relationship.

I have found that families who have received closure from the business of the death of a loved one often remain with one accord, spend time with each other, and keep in contact. This type of connection really helps to lighten the burden of grief.

Proper Distribution of Assets

Oh yes, when you have a plan, in most cases you don't have to worry about one sibling hiding the proceeds from everyone else. I say this in a joking way, but this really happens in families.

Having your affairs in order will provide clear instructions on how to distribute assets. Even when it boils down to items not listed—such as clothing, dishes, or family pictures—I have noticed that the sharing process usually turns out to be very cordial.

Time for Closure

When a loved one transitions, my wish is for family members to be at their bedside if that is their choice, not running around trying to figure out what to do.

Now that I've *Told You*, Let Me *Show You*

Doris Payne Jackson, my mom, was the first patron of *My Exit Plan.* She and I often talked through the details of what she did and did not want at the time of her death. Mom lived for fifteen years with multiple myeloma and multiple sclerosis. As sick as she was, she was determined not to leave a mess behind for her children to clean up. Her biggest concern was ensuring care for my oldest brother, who had a learning disability. I committed to taking care of him with my siblings' help. Her Plan spelled out her exact wishes.

When mom transitioned to her heavenly home, her Exit Plan became our guidebook. My mom's insurance policy and other important documents were well organized. We opened her estate and sold her home. Each of her five children received equal shares of her estate, and final accounting was completed, approved, and closed by the Register of Wills. Our process for handling her funeral service and closing out her estate went smoothly because mom had a Plan.

Elder Frank Grier was another benefactor of *My Exit Plan.* He and I met several times over a period of five years. He made sure to have his house in order when God called him home. It only took a phone call to start the ball rolling to ensure his Plan was complete. Because we had met often and combed through every detail, I could just about memorize who was supposed to do what for his homegoing service.

Several times, just when we thought we had the Plan complete, someone who was listed to participate in Elder Grier's funeral service would predecease him. This happened several times, and when it did, Elder Grier made sure he met with me within a day of the death notice of his friend in order to update his service program. He never wanted these discussions to take place over the phone—always in person. At times, I would be in my office meeting with another family when he'd tap on the door and say, "Elder Grier here ... just need to see you for a minute." When he realized there was someone in my office, he'd politely say, "Ooh, you're with a family. I'll just wait for you." And that's what he did. Once I was free, Elder Grier would revise his Plan, and we would carefully review the entire file just to make sure I was clear about what he wanted.

Elder Grier died on February 1, 2010. There was a snowstorm that day, and my team and I worked remotely day and night to arrange his funeral service and complete the program he'd laid out in his Exit Plan, which included his life story that he wrote. Everything was in place, and his service went off without a hitch! Everyone he designated to participate in his service was in place. There were no decisions to be made because he had made them all and discussed them with his wife and children prior to his death. His completed *My Exit Plan* allowed his family to grieve and say their final goodbyes without worrying about the many details surrounding his service or how to transition their lives after his death.

 **Juanita Waller**, a coworker and FBCG member, entered my office one day and said she wanted "to get her house in order!" She completed her Exit Plan, and a few weeks later performed in a skit demonstrating how important it was to have a Plan. Only God knew that shortly thereafter, Juanita would no longer be with us here on earth. We traveled to her hometown to meet her family and we were able to arrange her homegoing services based on her desires as detailed in her Exit Plan. Juanita was a dedicated member of Prosperity Partners, a ministry at the church that focuses on being debt free. The director of the ministry, Michelle Singletary, and other members traveled to her hometown to support the family as well.

John Bussie, a soft-spoken and gentle giant was the husband of my former coworker, Catherine Bussie. He was a loving husband, father, and grandfather who served as an usher at our church. His wife had attended one of my workshops on "getting your house in order," and shortly thereafter, John became ill. Catherine remembered the workshop and realized that they needed an Exit Plan.

I can vividly remember the day Catherine called and asked if we could meet to get their affairs in order. Within a few days, I met with both Catherine and John to complete their Plan. Because of the special love that John had for Catherine, he wanted to make sure everything was in order for her.

Then John's health began to decline, and he later transitioned. Because his wife knew everything he wanted, it only took a few hours to plan a wonderful celebration service for him. After the service, Catherine was able to grieve the death of her husband of forty-six years and eventually decide what she would do with the rest of her life. Catherine is grateful that she did not have to go to probate court to open an estate. They had their house in order!

Timothy and Janis Boyette, both faithful members of my church, were referred to me by Reverend Belynda Gentry in 2012. Janis was a very sweet, soft-spoken woman who knew what she wanted. She was diagnosed with ALS some years earlier, and her health was beginning to fail. Janis was very interested in completing her Exit Plan and encouraged her husband to complete his as well. I was so amazed when I met this couple, because they interviewed me. They wanted to know why the Exit Plan was so important to me. At the end of our meeting, they were at peace with their Exit Plan arrangements and could focus on living from that day on. Janis transitioned in 2013, and Timothy transitioned in 2017 from a heart condition. This experience of walking through two additional well-planned services encouraged me to continue moving forward with *My Exit Plan* and writing this book.

 **Wyllie Mitchell** and his wife, Lorna, both members of my church, were referred to me through someone at our church. Wyllie, known as "Mitch" to his family and friends, was experiencing health challenges at the time and was scheduled to have major surgery. Mitch wanted to make sure he had his papers in order in case he didn't make it through his surgery. I spoke to his wife Lorna on the phone and scheduled our meeting.

When the day of our meeting came, this giant of a man stood tall and was firm in his conversation. He wanted to plan his funeral from beginning to end, so we completed his program, including decisions about who would and would not speak. Mitch questioned me to make sure I was firm enough to carry out his wishes for his service. I spent the day with them, as he had to make other major decisions as well.

About a year and a half later, Mitch had his surgery, and God blessed him to make it through! Lorna said that once Mitch made his arrangements, he was at peace and was able to focus on his health. God allowed Mitch to spend the next two years with family before he transitioned. Having his Exit Plan proved to be a valuable asset for Mitch and his family. It allowed them to focus solely on celebrating his life once he transitioned rather than having to deal with the painful burden of planning for his services.

Chapter Six:
MAKING ARRANGEMENTS

PRE-ARRANGEMENTS

I strongly recommend you decide on your own pre-arrangements if there is a possibility that two or more family members may not agree. Having to make decisions on what funeral home to use and what cemetery to bury a loved one in at the time of death can be overwhelming. Pre-arrangements will allow your family to put into action what you have already put in place. Making your own decisions in advance removes the stress of your family having to come to an agreement.

As part of your decision-making, knowing the history of the funeral home is very important. A couple of questions you may want to ask are 1) how long has the funeral home been in business? and 2) how many families have they served in the past year? Do your homework!

LIFE INSURANCE

It is wise to review your insurance policies periodically. One complication that can occur is having your insurance company bought out by another company. Tracking down the new company can require a lot of work if the sale of the policy took place several years ago.

When all the beneficiaries have predeceased the policyholder, you must provide a death certificate for each person. You must then prove who their children are since they will become the next set of beneficiaries unless otherwise stated in a will. This type of situation can often be the cause of funds having to be included in probate versus being used immediately for the service.

If you do not have insurance and want to purchase some, several companies offer affordable insurance with no medical exams or decrease in benefits. They are often listed on Facebook, TV commercials, and the internet.

INSURANCE FOR INFANTS & CHILDREN UP TO AGES TWENTY-SIX

I pray that everyone with children either purchases a policy or adds their children to their own policy as a Child Rider on the day they are born. A Child Rider policy usually costs no more than one dollar a month! I have funeralized several children over the past two decades where the parents did not have insurance on the child. Some parents have used their savings or a credit card to pay for the service and burial and others have had to rely on donations. Unfortunately, babies transition just like adults. We must be prepared for the little ones too!

INSURANCE FOR ADULT CHILDREN AGES TWENTY-SIX AND OLDER

Young adults age out of parental policies at twenty-six years old. You should encourage them to purchase a policy either through their job or privately prior to their twenty-sixth birthday. If the young adult is listed as a rider on your policy, you should receive a letter indicating that he or she is aging out and that you need to purchase a policy.

REPATRIATION INSURANCE

People often wonder how to handle a situation when a loved one transitions miles away from the family home, whether they are visiting or living in another state. Until recently, I was concerned about the steps a family member would take in such a case. Then my granddaughter moved to Los Angeles to pursue her dream. After I recovered from the shock of her not having family in LA, I began to worry about what we would do if something happened to her while there. My comfort came from making sure we had a set of keys to her house, power of attorney, will, POD (paid on death) on her bank account, and an Exit Plan to carry out her wishes.

My granddaughter not only lives in a different state but, as a wardrobe stylist, she also frequently travels to various countries. Shipping a deceased loved one from another country can be very expensive and nerve-wracking. It can also take forever. So I researched purchasing Repatriation Insurance for when she travels abroad, and I learned that it will cover or at least defray the cost of the legal matters and returning your loved one back to the United States. This sounds like a lot, but for some people, it's worth it.

Prior to traveling abroad, you should check with your local government to see if there are any red flag warnings about traveling to that area. Also, visit the www.visitorsinsurancereviews.com for more information.[1]

What is Repatriation Insurance?

In the case of a death abroad, the costs, documentation, and customs negotiations necessary to retrieve the body and transport it safely back home can be astronomical. The responsibility of recovering a traveler's body, the return of their mortal remains, falls to the traveler's family, and the sheer effort of navigating the regulations of the foreign country - often in an unfamiliar language - can be overwhelming in an already difficult time.

Equally concerning are the costs of funerals abroad. Do you know whether your visitors insurance will cover a funeral abroad?

Visitors insurance is critical in the case of death in a foreign country. With adequate visitors insurance, the cost and effort of recovering your body from a foreign country will be managed by people who are experienced with the laws and regulations. Your family has enough stress in the case of a death overseas, and visitors insurance with benefits for repatriation of remains means they will not be responsible for the costs, negotiations, and other tasks associated with the complicated process of retrieving your body and returning it home for burial.

What is the cost of transporting a body?

According to travel experts, the cost of repatriation from the U.S. to Kenya, for example, can range anywhere from US $6,000 to US $10,000.

Paperwork requirements, medical costs, mortuary charges, and embalming fees vary widely from country to country. The cost of repatriating a body

---

1   Information from the Visitors Insurance Reviews website, https://www.visitorsinsurancereviews. com/visitors-insurance-company-reviews/

depends on two main factors: the distance to be traveled and fees levied by the surrendering and receiving governmental offices.

What about sending someone back home who is seriously injured or in danger?

For serious injuries and evacuation you'll need to have medical evacuation insurance. This type of insurance is very popular on events like cruises, where the nearest hospital on land may be hundreds of miles or more away. In case you're looking for this type of coverage consider reading more on Getting Rescued: Emergency Medical Evacuation.

What eligible expenses are included in repatriation?

Most visitors insurance plans are similar when it comes to the definition and coverage for repatriation of remains. Repatriation benefits are focused around the appropriate preparation and transportation of the deceased traveler back to their home country. As such, the eligible expenses include the following:

- Reasonable preparation of the body for transportation, including cremation or embalming, a minimally necessary container appropriate for transportation, shipping costs and the necessary governmental authorizations.
- Air or ground transportation of bodily remains or ashes to air or ground terminal nearest to the principal residence of the deceased.

Other important facts about return of mortal remains:

- The death must occur outside of the traveler's home country.
- The focus of repatriation coverage is isolated to the proper care and treatment of the body and its safe return to the traveler's home country.
- The repatriation must be coordinated and managed by the insurance company; any costs not approved or arranged by the insurance company will not be reimbursed.
- Costs for a domestic burial are not included with repatriation coverage in a visitors insurance plan, but many plans do cover the costs of a burial abroad.

Remember that repatriation can be very expensive, so it is important to consider the possibility of such incidents and select a policy maximum that would provide sufficient coverage.

A Portrait of A Friend

A dedication to
Cynthia Ann "Cyndi" Day

Cyndi died on May 30, 2019, while vacationing in the Dominican Republic.

If by chance I were called upon
To define a very true friend,
It wouldn't be hard, for I know of one
Who epitomized "friend" to the end.

It mattered not your walk in life
Nor your race, your color or creed,
If Cyndi met you, and sensed a void
She would do her best to meet every need.

No hour was too late nor road too long
For Cyndi to lend a hand;
She could calm the most distraught heart
With gentle words like "I understand."

We love you and will forever miss you,
Fond memories may even bring a tear,
As your laughter, smile, and compassion
Become reminiscences we'll always hold dear.

© Geneva Pearson

SELECTING A FUNERAL HOME

To me, selecting a funeral home is like shopping for a new hair stylist, barber, or makeup artist. I need to know the quality of the final presentation. In addition, I look for professional services to be rendered, and, as part of that, staff appearance and setup is very important. It is better not to make an appointment for a service until you know what type of service you want.

I have seen people select a funeral home because that was who their neighbor used, without knowing what their loved one was going to look like in the end and without knowing the quality of their work. On the day of the service, the family was distraught because the deceased looked nothing like themselves or because the makeup was very heavy. At that point, there is not a lot that can be done to change the appearance.

One day I met with a well-known mortician and absorbed her knowledge like a sponge. I wanted to know why some people look like they've died of shock and others look so peaceful. For instance, I attended one service where the hands of the deceased were protruding out of the casket rather than lying down on the body. I could not believe my eyes. My first thought was, *What funeral home would do something like this?* I also wanted to know what could be done about people with spastic limbs. I know that sometimes people have illnesses that cause spasticity, but I've seen morticians relax such limbs to the point where the person looked perfectly normal. The mortician I consulted with explained the process of massaging the limbs so that they would not protrude up or out; this was just as important to her as it was to me.

On a few occasions, prior to a service, I've rushed through, cleaning spots from suits or dresses on the deceased or requesting that makeup and hair be re-touched. Once again, to me, presentation is everything when it comes to a homegoing service. With modern technology and updated makeup, there is no reason for your loved one not to look their best. This is one of the reasons I tell people to make sure that you are using a funeral home with a good reputation!

It is also important to review all contracts line by line to make sure you are not signing to pay for a service that you did not request. You must also compare costs; high price is not necessarily the best quality. In many instances, *a la carte* can be more expensive than purchasing a package. Get what you need and what you can afford.

Not every funeral home is owned by the family name they go by. Never choose a funeral home because of a twenty-year-old relationship with them, or because the funeral home is in your neighborhood. Educate yourself!

SERVICE PREFERENCES

It is important to let your family know what type of service you desire. Here are a few options to consider for your final arrangements:

- Open casket, viewing, service, and burial
- Closed casket, visitation, service, and burial
- Open casket and viewing followed by cremation
- Direct cremation, memorial service
- Direct burial, graveside
- Memorial service – remains donated
- No service

Federal law requires that funeral homes provide you with a general price list before leaving your meeting with them. The itemized list provides details of every service the funeral home offers and how much each service costs. The number one reason people overpay is because they do not shop around prior to needing the service. Instead, they pick the closest funeral home or one that their family previously has used. By using resources such as the Red Book Funeral Directory or searching online, you can choose a funeral home in your area that will provide the opportunity to compare prices and services. These references can also be found online.

STANDARD CASKETS

If you choose a casket service, you may want to pre-select your casket or at least share with your loved ones what your preference is. That way your family will not have to debate over whether to purchase a sealed or non-sealed casket, color, or company. The more decisions you make in advance, the less chance of confusion and contention within your family later.

It is important to allow the funeral home to receive your loved one (after the transition), prior to your appointment to make arrangements and your purchases, so that they can determine what size casket is needed. You don't want to receive a call after your meeting saying that you need to change the casket and that the cost has increased.

OVERSIZED CASKETS

If you or your loved one's body frame is broad, you may need an oversized casket. The cost can increase over a thousand dollars. Make sure you budget for this upfront. Casket size may also affect the cost of the burial ground. An oversized casket can be wider than a standard casket and grave. You may need to purchase two sites and, in some cases, pay for two opening and closings depending on the cemetery.

TRANSPORTATION

If you plan to use limousines, decide who you plan to transport to the service and/or cemetery so that you will know how many cars to include in your package. You can also contract with a private limousine company for your transportation.

Out-of-State Burials

If you plan to have an out-of-state burial, include the cost of transportation to that location, a receiving fee for the funeral home in that state, and the burial cost.

Choosing a Cemetery

The cemetery selection is another area that can be rather costly. Purchasing your plot in advance can save your family money and the stress of having to make a quick decision in a short time frame. Families normally wish to place their loved ones close to one another. However, when you wait until a death occurs, usually most surrounding sites have been sold and are not available. What a disappointment!

Casket Liners and Vaults

Some states require by law to have an outer burial container for the casket. These are called liners or vaults. Many people do not know you can purchase a casket liner or vault from the funeral home for a great deal less than making the purchase at the cemetery. If you decide to do so, have this discussion upfront with the cemetery and the funeral home. IMPORTANT: If you or your loved one requires an oversized casket, this needs to be known upfront to assure that the liner or vault is the correct size and the grave is prepared for the correct measurements.

Headstones and Memorials

It is important to know what type of headstones or memorials are acceptable in the area where you purchase your plot. Families have called me in tears because they wanted an upright headstone but the area requires flat headstones. So what can you do? Either go through the expense of having your loved one exhumed to place them in an area where uprights are acceptable, or settle for a flat headstone. Also, know that you do not have to make your purchase at the cemetery. There are companies that offer beautiful headstones for reasonable prices.

Chapter Eight

DISPOSITION OF REMAINS

BURIAL PREFERENCES

There are several types of burials. Sharing this information will help your family make final decisions if you have not pre-planned.

- In Ground Burial
- Above Ground in a Community Mausoleum
- Above Ground in a Lawn Crypt
- Above Ground in a Private Mausoleum
- Inurnment or Interment of Ashes
- Green Burials

CREMATIONS

I can remember years ago when it was assumed that people who were cremated did not have the funds for a proper burial. Today, however, it's common for people to choose cremation. Some people do not want their family to spend a lot of money, and others do not want their remains above or below ground.

If cremation is your choice, please put it in writing so that your spouse, children, or significant other will not be accused of making that decision on their own for financial reasons. Also make it known what you want done with your ashes. Who will be the keeper of the ashes? Today, some families are making jewelry pieces from the ashes to share them with one another.

Organ Donation

If you have decided to be an organ donor, make sure you have registered to do so. Failing to register could result in a delay for your family and/or not being accepted as a donor. Registration for organ donations can be done at your local department of motor vehicles or online at www.organdonor.gov. Please make sure you clearly articulate what organs you wish to donate. Lastly, share your decision with your family.

Whole Body Donation

Many people choose to donate their body to medical schools for research and training. I would suggest that you check with your state anatomy board for a program in your area and for registration information.

I would also share the information with immediate family so that they will know what to do when the time comes.

Chapter Nine

WHAT IS NEEDED TO COMPLETE A SERVICE

DEATH CERTIFICATES

The information that the funeral director will ask you for in order to complete an application for a death certificate can be found in *My Exit Plan*. You can also determine how many certificates will be needed based on assets and information listed.

The information given for a death certificate will go on a vital statistics form. Double-check the form before you leave the funeral home to make sure the information is correct. And make sure you review the death certificate as soon as you receive it. If there are errors, you can have it amended at no cost in most areas, depending on the local state rules and regulations. Submitting a death certificate with incorrect information could delay payment of insurance.

Make sure that you purchase a death certificate for each insurance company as well as each bank, mortgage company, employer, and any other funding source, to include Social Security, Office of Personnel Management, Veterans Affairs, etc. Also, keep one for your records. You may need it years down the road.

You should also send a copy of the death certificate to the following credit bureaus so that they will be aware of the death and close the credit accounts for your loved one. This will make sure that new accounts cannot be opened in their name. Please call to find out what other documents you will need to send.

Experian

PO Box 9701
Allen, Texas 75013
888-397-3742

Equifax

PO BOX 105069
Atlanta, GA 30348
800-525-6285

Transunion

PO BOX 2000
Chester, PA 19016-2000
800-680-7289

PROGRAMS

Some people desire to have a simple funeral program, while others prefer a book with lots of pictures. Choose your favorite poems, and keep your old childhood photos—along with a draft of what you would like—in a safe place known to your family. If you wish for your family to be responsible for your program, make sure you tell them when discussing your Exit Plan to provide more than enough copies. Everyone who attends the service should receive a program.

To accommodate our members, we can accept a Dropbox file or an external drive with the program and/or obituary that has been prepared.

SERVICE PARTICIPANTS

Make a list of people you want to include as a participant in the service. Replace people who have passed away. Also, if you know you have a family member or friend who is long-winded, that might not be the person to choose to give remarks.

WHAT YOUR FAMILY SHOULD KNOW

Sharing your likes and dislikes with your family can be very helpful. I remember two sisters feuding over what color their mom was going to wear. One sibling said that the deceased did not like pink, while the other insisted on purchasing pink. So, they went around and around until one spouse said, "Just use black!"

Putting your desires in writing should help eliminate the drama of the family having to assume what you would want. People have told me specifics such as they want their eyeglasses on, hair in braids, a certain style wig, or a clean-shaven haircut.

OBITUARIES

When it comes to the obituary and newspaper, no one knows better than the deceased who they would like to list. The discussion has often surfaced about ex-spouses and/or deceased spouses: Do you list the ex when there were children between the two? What do you do when there is a new spouse? What if the ex-spouse remarried? How about when there have been multiple spouses—do you list them all? Do you list the stepchildren if the deceased did not have a relationship with them? Just where do you draw the line?

Good questions! If you answer them now, your family will not have to wonder.

POLICIES OF THE CHURCH AND OTHER VENUES

Knowing your church policy—what they offer and what is acceptable—is very important. Having to search for a place at the last minute to have a service can be taxing.

I have learned over the years that families will contact and visit the funeral home, cemetery, and florist and then contact the church with an expectation that everything will work together for the date that they have already scheduled. I work at a large church, and there are days that we have had two services a day. On more than one occasion, a service was already confirmed for the date the family requested. And when a call comes in for a funeral, I cannot always give an available date during the initial call; I must check the sanctuary schedule to make sure nothing is scheduled to take place on the requested date.

In some areas, churches allow the casket to remain open during the entire service. In others, the casket may be closed before the service and re-opened at the end of the service for a final viewing. Many churches, however, do not re-open caskets after the initial viewing; once the service starts, the casket remains closed.

Many churches do not allow any type of organizational rituals during the service. They have policies on who can preach the eulogy and how long the service will last. You need to know this upfront.

If you are planning to bring in a musician with or without equipment, you want to be clear about what equipment you can use and what you can or cannot connect to, such as amplifiers.

And in the event that you have more than one loved one being funeralized at the same time, you want to make sure the church is staffed to handle the request.

Different cultures have different understandings of the eulogy versus the obituary; some, for instance, are accustomed to long services and repasts. You want to make sure that the church clearly understands your requests and that you understand their policy.

POLICIES FOR FUNERAL HOMES

In my twenty-plus years of doing funerals, I have never had a funeral home be disrespectful or abusive to my teams. However, there are funeral homes that choose to do whatever they desire while working a service. So, I make it my business to contact the funeral home prior to the service to make sure we are both proceeding with one accord. There are some things that we do not allow during services, and we make that clear upfront.

If the funeral home has never carried out a service at your location, they will need to know when to do the final viewing with the family, when to close the casket, and, in some cases, whether or not to reopen the casket after the service. They will also need to know whether the final viewing is done from the current location of the casket or if you would allow the funeral home to roll the casket before the family. Also, it is very important to know if they have planned to add something to the service that is not on the program.

Chapter Ten:
FILING FOR BENEFITS

Office of Personnel Management, Social Security, and Veterans Affairs

If your loved one was receiving social security prior to their death, you should contact your local office to determine if any additional benefits will be paid out after their death. If they were a government or private business employee, you should contact the office of human resources for their job.

Several years ago, I ran into a mother of five children whose spouse had passed away. She received his government benefits but did not know that the family was entitled to social security benefits. I ran into her a year later only to discover that she had never applied for social security benefits for herself or her children. We made a phone call, and, to her surprise, in a little over a month, she received a check for back payment of benefits. This family was fewer than thirty days away from losing their home. The lump sum check allowed her to bring her mortgage current and pay all her bills that were overdue. What a blessing for the family!

OFFICE OF PERSONNEL MANAGEMENT[2]

Deceased Employees Covered Under FERS (Federal Employees Retirement System)

BASIC EMPLOYEE DEATH BENEFIT

Surviving Spouse

If an employee dies with at least 18 months of creditable civilian service under FERS, a survivor annuity may be payable if:

- the surviving spouse was married to the deceased for at least nine months, or
- the employee's death was accidental, or

---

2   Information from the Office of Personnel Management website, www.opm.gov

- there was a child born of the marriage to the employee.

The spouse may be eligible for the Basic Employee Death Benefit, which is equal to 50% of the employee's final salary (average salary, if higher), plus $15,000 (increased by Civil Service Retirement System cost-of-living adjustments beginning 12/1/87). The $15,000 has increased to $32,423.56 for deaths after December 1, 2016.

Former Spouse

The Basic Employee Death Benefit may be payable to a former spouse (in whole or in part), if a qualifying court order, awarding a benefit, is on file at OPM and the former spouse was married to the deceased for a total of at least nine months and did not remarry before reaching age 55.

MONTHLY SURVIVOR BENEFITS

Surviving Spouse

If a FERS employee dies, recurring monthly payments may be made to the surviving spouse if the deceased employee completed at least 10 years of creditable service (18 months of which must be civilian service)

To qualify for the monthly benefit the surviving spouse must have been married to the employee for at least nine months.

If the death occurred before nine months, a survivor annuity may still be payable if:

- the employee's death was accidental, or
- there was a child born of the marriage.

Former Spouse

Recurring monthly payments may be made to the former spouse of a deceased employee under a court order. A former spouse must also meet the nine month marriage requirement. For additional information about court-ordered benefits, refer to the pamphlet, 'Court-Ordered Benefits for Former Spouses (PDF file) on the website.'

Children

Unmarried children who are dependent upon the employee may receive monthly benefits until they reach age 18, marry, or die. Monthly survivor annuity payments for a child can continue after age 18, if the child is a full-time student attending a recognized school. Benefits can continue until age 22.

Unmarried disabled dependent children may receive recurring monthly benefits, if the disability occurred before age 18.

We consider a child dependent if he/she:

- was born of the marriage to the retiree;
- is an adopted child who meets all of the following conditions-
- the child lived with the deceased retiree, and
- the deceased filed a petition to adopt the child, and
- the child was adopted by the surviving spouse after the retiree died.
- Is a stepchild or recognized child born out of wedlock who was living with the retiree in a parent-child relationship when the retiree died; or
- Is a recognized child born out of wedlock for whom a judicial determination of support has been obtained.

We consider the child dependent if there is proof that the deceased made regular and substantial contributions to the child's support.

The combined benefit of all the children is reduced by the total amount of child's insurance benefits that are payable (or would, upon proper application, be payable) under Title II of the Social Security Act for the same month to all children of the deceased (including those of a former marriage who may not be living with the current spouse) based on the total earnings of the deceased. In many cases, the FERS children's benefit is reduced to $0.

Lump Sum Benefits

If no survivor annuity is payable upon the employee/former employee's death, a lump sum may be payable of the unpaid balance of retirement contributions made by the employee. This lump sum is payable under the order of precedence.

Death of a Former Federal Employee Under FERS

Monthly Survivor Annuity

Surviving Spouse

If a former employee who dies with at least 10 years of creditable service (5 years of which must be creditable civilian service) is survived by a spouse who was married to the deceased at the time of his/her separation from Federal civilian service AND who:

- was married to the deceased for at least nine months, or
- the former employee's death was accidental, or
- there was a child born of the marriage to the former employee;

the spouse may be eligible for a monthly survivor benefit. The benefit begins on the date the deceased former employee would have been eligible for an unreduced annuity, unless the survivor chooses to have it begin at a lower rate on the day after the employee's death. The former employee would have been eligible for an unreduced annuity with a minimum of 10 years of creditable service and less than 20 years of service at age 62, with 20 or more years of service at age 60, or with 30 years of service at his/her Minimum Retirement Age (MRA), according to the schedule found on the website.

Instead of a survivor annuity, the eligible spouse can elect to receive a lump sum payment of the contributions remaining to the deceased person's credit in the retirement fund.

Former Spouse

The monthly survivor benefit may be paid in whole or in part to a former spouse if a qualifying court order is on file at OPM and it awards a benefit.

Children

No monthly benefits are payable to children of deceased former FERS employees if the death occurs after leaving Federal employment under FERS and before retirement.

Lump Sum Benefit

If a former employee dies and no survivor annuity is payable, the retirement contributions remaining to the deceased person's credit in the Civil Service Retirement and Disability Fund, plus applicable interest, are payable. This lump sum is payable under the order of precedence.

SOCIAL SECURITY[3]

How Social Security Can Help You When a Family Member Dies

You should let Social Security know as soon as possible when a person in your family dies. Usually, the funeral director will report the person's death to Social Security. You'll need to give the deceased's Social Security number to the funeral director so they can make the report.

Some of the deceased's family members may be able to receive Social Security benefits if the deceased person worked long enough in jobs insured under Social Security to qualify for benefits. Contact Social Security as soon as you can to make sure the family gets all the benefits they're entitled to. Please read the following information carefully to learn what benefits may be available.

- We can pay a one-time payment of $255 to the surviving spouse if they were living with the deceased. If living apart and eligible for certain Social Security benefits on the deceased's record, the surviving spouse may still be able to get this one-time payment. If there's no surviving spouse, a child who's eligible for benefits on the deceased's record in the month of death can get this payment.
- Certain family members may be eligible to receive monthly benefits, including:
- A widow or widower age 60 or older (age 50 or older if disabled);
- A widow or widower any age caring for the deceased's child who is under age 16 or disabled;
    - ◊ An unmarried child of the deceased who is:
        - Younger than age 18 (or up to age 19 if they're a full-time student in an elementary or secondary school); or
        - Age 18 or older with a disability that began before age 22;
    - ◊ A stepchild, grandchild, step-grandchild, or adopted child under certain circumstances;
    - ◊ Parents, age 62 or older, who were dependent on the deceased for at least half of their support; and
    - ◊ A surviving divorced spouse, under certain circumstances.

If the deceased was receiving Social Security benefits, you must return the benefit received for the month of death or any later months. For example, if the person dies in July, you must return the benefit paid in August. If received by direct deposit, contact the bank or other financial institution and ask them to

---

3   Information from the Social Security Administration website, https://www.ssa.gov/onlineservices/

return any funds received for the month of death or later. If paid by check, do not cash any checks received for the month the person dies or later. Return the checks to Social Security as soon as possible.

However, eligible family members may be able to receive death benefits for the month the beneficiary died.

Contacting Social Security

The most convenient way to contact us anytime, anywhere is to visit www.socialsecurity.gov. There, you can: apply for benefits; open a my Social Security account, which you can use to review your Social Security Statement, verify your earnings, print a benefit verification letter, change your direct deposit information, request a replacement Medicare card, and get a replacement SSA-1099/1042S; obtain valuable information; find publications; get answers to frequently asked questions; and much more.

If you don't have access to the internet, we offer many automated services by telephone, 24 hours a day, 7 days a week. Call us toll-free at 1-800-772-1213 or at our TTY number, 1-800-325-0778, if you're deaf or hard of hearing.

If you need to speak to a person, we can answer your calls from 7 a.m. to 7 p.m., Monday through Friday. We ask for your patience during busy periods since you may experience a higher than usual rate of busy signals and longer hold times to speak to us. We look forward to serving you.

Form Approved
OMB No. 0960-0013

APPLICATION FOR LUMP-SUM DEATH PAYMENT*

I apply for all insurance benefits for which I am eligible under Title II (Federal Old-Age, Survivors, and Disability Insurance) of the Social Security Act, as presently amended, on the named deceased's Social Security record.

(This application must be filed within 2 years after the date of death of the wage earner or self-employed person.)

* This may also be considered an application for insurance benefits payable under the Railroad Retirement Act.

1.	(a) PRINT name of Deceased Wage Earner or Self-Employed Person (herein referred to as the "deceased")	FIRST NAME, MIDDLE INITIAL, LAST NAME
	(b) Check (X) one for the deceased	☐ Male ☐ Female
	(c) Enter deceased's Social Security Number	
2.	PRINT your name	FIRST NAME, MIDDLE INITIAL, LAST NAME
3.	Enter date of birth of deceased *(Month, day, year)*	
4.	(a) Enter date of death *(Month, day, year)*	
	(b) Enter place of death *(City and State)*	
5.	(a) Did the deceased ever file an application for Social Security benefits, a period of disability under Social Security, supplemental security income, or hospital or medical insurance under Medicare?	☐ Yes *(If "Yes," answer (b) and (c).)* ☐ No ☐ Unknown *(If "No" or "Unknown," go on to item 6.)*
	(b) Enter name(s) of person(s) on whose Social Security record(s) other application was filed.	FIRST NAME, MIDDLE INITIAL, LAST NAME
	(c) Enter Social Security Number(s) of person(s) named in (b). (If unknown, so indicate)	
6.	ANSWER ITEM 6 **ONLY** IF THE DECEASED WORKED WITHIN THE PAST 2 YEARS.	
	(a) About how much did the deceased earn from employment and self-employment during the year of death?	AMOUNT $
	(b) About how much did the deceased earn the year before death?	AMOUNT $
7.	ANSWER ITEM 7 **ONLY** IF THE DECEASED DIED PRIOR TO AGE 66 AND WITHIN THE PAST 4 MONTHS.	
	(a) Was the deceased unable to work because of illness, injuries or conditions at the time of death?	☐ Yes *(if "Yes," answer (b).)* ☐ No *(If "No," go on to item 8.)*
	(b) Enter the date the deceased became unable to work *(Month, day, year)*	
8.	(a) Was the deceased in the active military or naval service (including Reserve or National Guard active duty or active duty for training) after September 7, 1939 and before 1968?	☐ Yes *(If "Yes," answer (b) and (c).)* ☐ No *(If "No," go on to item 9.)*
	(b) Enter dates of service.	From: *(Month, Year)* To: *(Month, Year)*
	(c) Has anyone (including the deceased) received, or does anyone expect to receive, a benefit from any other Federal agency?	☐ Yes ☐ No
9.	Did the deceased work in the railroad industry for 7 years or more?	☐ Yes ☐ No

Form **SSA-8** (11-2013) EF (11-2013)   Page 1
Destroy Prior Editions

Figure 1 - Social Security Lump Sum Death Payment Application

Veterans Affairs[4]

When a Military Service Member or Retiree Dies

If your spouse was a member of the Armed Forces, there are several steps to take to ensure you have alerted the proper agencies. You should also be aware of the various spousal benefits for which you may qualify. If you are claiming benefits as the surviving spouse, you will have to provide a copy of your marriage license. There are several departments you must notify when a military service member or retiree dies. They are listed below:

- **Personnel Center.** Depending on the branch of service, the Personnel Center that maintains the decedent's records will have to be notified. For example, if the person was in the US Air Force, the Air Force Personnel Center should be notified.

- **Defense Finance and Accounting Services (DFAS).** Service members and retirees are paid through DFAS. You will need to provide the decedent's social security number, date of death, and perhaps a copy of the death certificate.

- **US Department of Veterans Affairs (VA).** The VA will send a package of benefits forms and information to the surviving spouse. Carefully review the package and follow the instructions meticulously. Complete and return the forms to the appropriate locations listed on each form. Always keep a copy for your records; you will probably need it later to follow up on status updates and to ask related questions.

- **Defense Enrollment Eligibility Reporting System (DEERS).** DEERS will contact the TRICARE healthcare system to alert them of the death. If you are the deceased person's spouse and you were enrolled in TRICARE, you are likely eligible to maintain your healthcare through TRICARE. Note that TRICARE will typically send a letter of sympathy and provide critical information about coverage if you are the surviving spouse. If you are enrolled in TRICARE for healthcare or dental coverage, you will not need to change your coverage, but you may need to arrange for continued payment on the account if premiums were paid from your spouse's paycheck.

- **United States Automobile Association (USAA).** If you are insured (car or home) or have accounts with USAA, who provides products that are designed for military families, it is a good idea to also call them. It is likely that some of the products you use through USAA will need to be adjusted.

- **Local military ID card office.** When a service member transitions, the surviving spouse must exchange his/her existing military ID card for a widow(er) card. This process is simple. Make an appointment with your local ID card office located on a military installation. If your ID is soon to expire, they will replace your dependent card with a widow(er) card.

---

4   Information from the Veterans Affairs website, https://www.va.gov/

If you still have several months or more until your ID card expires, they may allow you to keep the card until you are nearing the expiration date. Note that nearly everyone you talk with will ask for a copy of the death certificate and/or your marriage license if applicable. It is a good idea to keep an electronic copy of the short death certificate, long death certificate, and marriage license on hand. You will need them often.

Burial Benefits

If you would like to have a military ceremony, contact the VA for an application for burial benefits. There are several burial-related allowances for which you may be eligible, including plot, interment, transportation expenses, etc. The VA will provide you with proper forms and details related to specific benefits.

Department of Veterans Affairs

INSTRUCTIONS FOR COMPLETING APPLICATION FOR BURIAL BENEFITS
(UNDER 38 U.S.C., CHAPTER 23)

IMPORTANT - READ THESE INSTRUCTIONS CAREFULLY

PRIVACY ACT INFORMATION: The responses you submit are considered confidential (38 U.S.C. 5701). They may be disclosed outside the Department of Veterans Affairs (VA) only if the disclosure is authorized under the Privacy Act, including the routine uses identified in the VA system of records, 58VA21/22/28, Compensation, Pension, Education and Vocational Rehabilitation and Employment Records - VA, published in the Federal Register. The requested information is considered relevant and necessary to determine maximum benefits under the law and is required to obtain benefits. Information submitted is subject to verification through computer matching programs with other agencies.

RESPONDENT BURDEN: We need this information to determine your eligibility to burial benefits. Title 38, United States Code, allows us to ask for this information. We estimate that you will need an average of 15 minutes to review the instructions, find the information, and complete this form. VA cannot conduct or sponsor a collection of information unless a valid OMB control number is displayed. Valid OMB control numbers can be located on the OMB Internet Page at **www.reginfo.gov/public/do/PRAMain**. If desired, you can call 1-800-827-1000 to get information on where to send comments or suggestions about this form.

1. GENERAL

   a. ELIGIBILITY - NON-SERVICE-CONNECTED

      (1) NON-SERVICE-CONNECTED BURIAL ALLOWANCE - A one-time payment for a veteran who was receiving VA pension or disability compensation; would have been receiving disability compensation but for the receipt of military retired pay, or had an eligible pending claim at the time of death.

      (2) SERVICE-CONNECTED BURIAL ALLOWANCE - A one-time payment for a veteran who was rated totally disabled for a service-connected disability or disabilities; excluding individual unemployability, or who died of a service-connected disability.

      (3) VA MEDICAL CENTER DEATH BURIAL ALLOWANCE - A one-time payment for a veteran whose death was not service-connected and who died while hospitalized by VA.

   b. BURIAL ALLOWANCE - A one-time benefit payment payable toward the expenses of the funeral and burial of the veteran's remains. Burial includes all legal methods of disposing of the veteran's remains including, but not limited to, cremation, burial at sea, and medical school donation.

   c. PLOT OR INTERMENT ALLOWANCE - A one-time benefit payment payable toward:

      (1) Expenses incurred for the plot or interment if burial was not in a national cemetery or other cemetery under the jurisdiction of the United States; OR

      (2) Expenses payable to a State (or political subdivision of a State) if the veteran died from non-service-connected causes and was buried in a State-owned cemetery or section used solely for the remains of persons eligible for burial in a national cemetery.

   "Plot" means the final disposition site of the remains, whether it is a grave, mausoleum vault, columbarium niche, or similar place. "Interment" means the burial of casketed remains in the ground or the placement of cremated remains into a columbarium niche.

   d. TRANSPORTATION EXPENSES - The cost of transporting the body to the place of burial may be paid in addition to the burial allowance when:

      (1) The veteran died of a service-connected disability or had a compensable service-connected disability and burial is in a national cemetery; OR

      (2) The veteran died while in a hospital, domiciliary or nursing home to which he/she had been properly admitted under authority of VA; OR

      (3) The veteran died en route while traveling under prior authorization of VA for the purpose of examination, treatment; OR

      (4) The veteran's remains are unclaimed and burial is in a national cemetery.

Figure 2 - Instructions for VA Burial Benefits Form

Pensions

If you are entitled to receive a surviving spouse's pension, you can arrange to make a Declaration of Status of Dependents (Form 21-686c) through the VA. Send your claims correspondence to the appropriate pension office that services your state (for example, the state of Maryland is serviced by the Claims Intake Center in Philadelphia, Pennsylvania).

You are your own advocate. Stay engaged with and in contact with the various agencies you will need to call. Get names of everyone you speak with, and take good notes. Call often, and ask questions. Beware that sometimes the process can take months or longer.

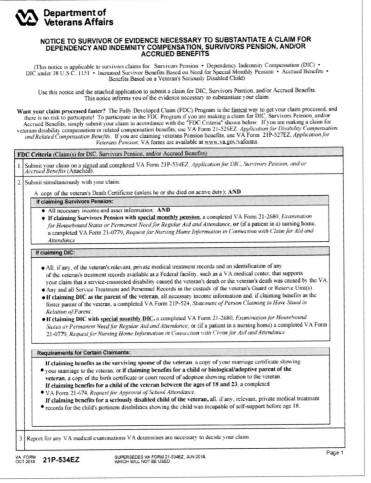

Figure 3 - VA Survivor Benefits Form

Chapter Eleven:
WHEN DEATH OCCURS AT HOME

WHEN HOSPICE IS INVOLVED

If you or your loved one is under hospice care, the first step to take after death is to contact the hospice nurse. He or she will have the next of kin contact the funeral home of choice. The funeral home will ask to speak to the nurse, after receiving location information from the next of kin. The funeral home will then arrive to remove the body.

If the police or ambulance is called, be sure to have the folder with all the important paperwork readily available to be viewed. This will determine whether your loved one will be transported to the hospital. I've had cases where the folder could not be found, and since admission to hospice could not be verified, the person was taken to the nearest hospital.

WHEN HOSPICE IS NOT INVOLVED

If you or your loved one is not under hospice, the first step to take after death is to contact the local police department. Let them know that someone has passed away in the home. In most cases, they will send paramedics to confirm the death, and the police will arrive to initiate an investigation to make sure there was no foul play. At some point, the police will contact the medical examiner to determine if the death was of natural causes. The deceased will either be released to the funeral home or sent to the medical examiner for further examination to determine the cause of death. Please note that in some cases, the police will ask everyone to leave the home until a decision has been made by the medical examiner.

I recently encountered a situation where a young man lived by himself and transitioned at home alone. His coworkers became concerned because it was not like him to not show up for work and not call. When the coworkers arrived at his home, they called the police because his vehicle was there, and he did not answer the door. In this case, no one within the local vicinity had a key, and his family lived hours away. In order to get keys and legally gain entry to his residence, his family had to go to probate court to file for letters of administration and present a death certificate to police. You may be asking, "Why is this so important?" They had to enter his home to get clothes for the service, insurance policies, and other important documents.

HOME REMOVALS

I have been at the home of several removals, and I suggest that family leave the room during the removal process. I also ask the removal service attendants to not cover the face of the loved one until they pass the family and exit the home. This allows family members to give their last kiss before their loved one leaves home.

> *"Recognizing that this earth is not our final resting place and that we all will die one day, it is only fair to your loved ones that you take the responsibility of providing them with your desires and the necessary information to make your arrangements when God calls you to your final resting place."*

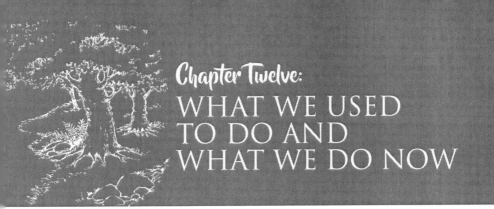

Chapter Twelve:
WHAT WE USED TO DO AND WHAT WE DO NOW

FUNERALS THEN VERSUS NOW

Years ago, all I had to do was contact the preacher to give the eulogy, the minister of music to lead the choir, and the catering manager to serve fried chicken. Then I had to search for the praying hands graphic to go with the obituary that was written by the family. With that, the program was complete. Whether the family had enough insurance to cover the service and burial, if there was a will, or how to process through grief, never came up.

WHERE WE ARE NOW – MOVING FORWARD

God showed me that there was more involved in serving bereaved families. We needed to move beyond the days of just planning the service for members. Families need much more than preparation for the day of service. They need end-to-end care and attention. For example, if the deceased does not have insurance, and the family does not have money for a service, my department will provide and discuss a list of options. The family can then bring closure to their loved one's transition.

It is my heart's desire to educate as many people as possible about these matters so that families are equipped with valuable information to make informed decisions. As a funeral manager, my desire is to assist families with aftercare, to include applying for benefits to get their household back to a manageable degree of normalcy.

OPENING AN ESTATE

If you know that your loved one has property and/or bank accounts solely in their name, and the property is not listed in a trust or the bank account does not have a beneficiary listed, you should plan to make a trip to your local

Register of Wills office to open an estate. With or without a will, this visit will be necessary.

In order to open an estate, you must have the will, if there is one. You must also have the death certificate, bank statements, documentation for the value of the property, funeral and burial bill, and any other related invoices. If you have paid bills (mortgage, gas, electric, water, phone, etc.) on behalf of the deceased, please keep records of all receipts and invoices so that you can be reimbursed.

If the bank statements are not available at the time of application, you may receive a limited letter that will allow you to only go to the bank to get statements to give to the court.

Depending on the value of the estate, the personal representative may need to be bonded and/or retain an attorney. Once the estate is opened, the personal representative will receive letters of administration that will allow you to close out all bank accounts and open an estate account.

It is important to know that you are not to use the credit cards or write checks for an account if you are not the co-applicant on that account. You should not take or distribute any funds or personal property of the deceased prior to approval from the court. The only funds that should come out of the estate account are for payments related to the deceased. Any refunds or monies due to the decedent and received after their death, should be payable to the estate account. If the decedent is receiving a social security and/or retirement check, the family or Personal Representative should call the office immediately to report the death. If your loved one transitions on the 15th of March and a check is received in April, you may have to return those funds. It's better to know this upfront than to have to pay the money back later.

I suggest to everyone that they list the person or persons they would like to serve as their personal representative. This will eliminate having to decide who will take on this task. It is important to know that if the person you designate has a criminal background, they may not be appointed.

You must open the estate in the jurisdiction where the deceased person lived. Please note that policies and procedures vary from state to state.

Chapter Thirteen: TESTIMONIALS

A BLESSING TO OUR FAMILY

Rhonda Green is an angel and a force to be reckoned with. She went above and beyond the call of duty for our family when our loved ones passed. We honestly had no idea what to do, what to set up, or who to call while grieving unimaginable losses.

For me personally, losing my grandparents were two of the most difficult situations I have ever had to deal with. For my wife, Nichole, losing her father recently has been devastating. Neither of us could handle all the details and challenges that naturally came up. There was just so much to do and so many things to handle. Rhonda was patient and gave us critical information to make the right decisions that we would be able to find peace with later.

From insurance to handling the details, Rhonda helped us make better decisions and guard ourselves against companies who almost pride themselves on taking advantage of families during the hardest times in their lives. She made the transition so much easier so we could focus on the grieving process and love on our family. That type of assistance isn't just work, it's a gift she has been given, and it's truly invaluable.

Thank you for everything you do!

Sincerely,

Etan & Nichole Thomas

A Gift That Keeps on Giving

It has been my utmost joy and admiration to witness Rhonda Green's vision of writing her first book unfold. It will undoubtedly prove to be an invaluable gift to many that keeps on giving! The beauty of her journey is that the evolution of this masterpiece embodies Rhonda's journey of what it means to be gifted and obediently walk in your destiny. It was through that obedience that the pages of this book were written as she used her God-given talent and undeniable gift!

Through our conversations, prayer calls and personal sister-friend moments, I can attest to the countless phone calls she's taken without hesitation or the times she's had to drop everything and run to her office to assist a family in need. She has certainly been a true blessing to me and my family during our time of bereavement.

Rhonda gracefully helps families with their Exit Plans and assists them during the most difficult times of their lives, with deep passion, extensive knowledge, and professionalism. What would take most to accomplish with a team, Rhonda quite often single-handedly performs alone and at tornadic speed! She walks together with families from the moment she receives an initial call, and she coordinates multiple resources to prepare programs and oversee homegoing celebrations. Her warm and inviting spirit and profound discernment to know when and how to respond to various situations and families never cease to amaze me!

Not only is this book a gift, but Rhonda also is a gift wrapped in a bow of love, which she exudes in everything she does. She is a prayer warrior who offers comfort and reassurance, a voice of reasoning amid confusion, a ray of sunshine in a room of darkness and for many simply an answer to prayers.

I'm so proud of you, Rhonda, for taking this huge step, and it is my prayer that God continues to richly bless you to take your vision to even higher heights!

Love you,

Nicole D. Graves

An Exit Plan Blessing

In the spring of 2011, my husband—the late Wyllie Mitchell, Jr.—was diagnosed with a lung disease. We were told by the doctors to get our affairs in order because if he received a lung transplant, he might die, and if he did not receive the transplant, he would die. Not having any experience in this area, I contacted FBCG to find out the procedure if something were to happen. I was forwarded to Ms. Rhonda Green, who scheduled an appointment to meet us at home, at which time she introduced my husband and I to "My Exit Plan," and before leaving she prayed a powerful prayer. Ms. Green informed us that by completing "My Exit Plan", he would be able to concentrate on living, knowing that arrangements were in place. I was very proud of my husband, who was very open and honest regarding how he wanted things to be carried out in the event of his death. (Side note: He comes from a family with "takeover spirit" and wanted to be certain that his wishes were carried out exactly how he wanted them.) We were given the forms, and it took us approximately a week to complete.

For the next three years, we were able to focus on Wyllie's treatments, doctors' appointments, hospitalizations—and there were many. In October 2012, he received a lung transplant and although he experienced many chronic rejections, the Exit Plan allowed him to concentrate on his treatment and health. On Sunday, November 16, 2014, God called him home, and knowing that Ms. Green was busy with Pastor and Church Anniversary, I informed her right before the service started, and she assured me that she would get on it. Ms. Green is very detail-oriented, and not only did she take care of crossing every "t" and dotting every "i" written in "My Exit Plan", she was very compassionate during the entire process. In all honesty, I don't believe she slept for days leading up to Mr. Mitchell's Homegoing Service.

My husband's Exit Plan was such a blessing to me; I have no idea what I would have done without it and Ms. Green. I am in the process now of completing my very own Exit Plan.

There are not enough words to express how grateful I am for Ms. Green and her obedience to God, for not thinking it robbery to share her gift with us.

To God be the glory, for all He has done.

Lorna Mitchell

It All Happened So Fast

On December 4, 2012, my husband Bryan Graham, Sr. was involved in a car accident. He was taken to Prince George's Hospital. I arrived at the hospital at approximately 4:00 p.m. and inquired as to his status. From 4:00 p.m. to approximately 8:00 p.m., I sat with no updates from anyone. My sister, Nicole Graves, and Rhonda Green were there supporting me as well. Upon seeing how upset I was, Rhonda found a doctor to tell us something. My husband had suffered severe head trauma. I could see him, albeit briefly, for a few minutes later that night.

On a related note, Rhonda called on prayer warriors at FBCG, and my brother-in-law, Rossie Graves, called on prayer warriors at Shiloh Baptist Church. You see, I repeatedly called my pastor, sent emails, and had other friends call on pastors at my church as well. No one from my church ever called, but I can honestly say that my extended church family from FBCG and Shiloh were there with me/us every step of the way, every day.

Unfortunately, on December 8, 2012, my husband succumbed to his injuries. After much prayer, I decided to have the funeral in Leesburg, Florida, our hometown. The funeral was scheduled for December 15, 2012. I had so much to do: Find a funeral home. (This was probably the easiest of all tasks. Rhonda Green had a relationship with the funeral home that other members of my family had used.) I had to provide clothing for Bryan to travel and clothing for the service. I had to make sure his body was released and prepared to go to Florida.

This proved to be a cumbersome task. Rhonda made this a seamless process for me. Not only did she call on friends in the right places to get the needed police report, she also stepped in for me to make sure that the funeral home had my hubby looking like himself. You see, the body wasn't released until Tuesday, December 11th, and I was already en route to Florida. She personally viewed the body prior to it being shipped to Florida. She told the mortician what changes needed to be made.

My next step was to prepare the obituary. This was done by my sister Nicole, with assistance from friends and family. A priceless gift that I will forever treasure.

Finally, I had left for Florida and Rhonda assured me that my husband's body would be in Florida no later than Thursday, December 13th and sure enough, he arrived on time.

So, Rhonda, I thank you, my family thanks you, and we appreciate everything that you did to make the journey a little less painful, a little less stressful, and a little more comforting. We love you and are honored to have you in our lives.

Again, thank you for all you do.

Sharri Graham

A JOB WELL DONE

The best-laid plans in life can never prepare one to handle the death of a loved one. Our mother passed away on October 4, 2015, and everything around us was frozen in place because the glue that held the family together took her last breath. We are a small family that was suddenly faced with the task of planning funeral and burial arrangements with little hands-on experience. It was during this time we met Rhonda, who is an attractive, professional, and personable individual with a wealth of hands-on experience in this arena. She volunteered to meet with our family to share some of her experiences with other families in similar situations. She briefed us on what to expect and offered helpful suggestions based on best practices to facilitate the grieving process. She consulted with individual members of the family to satisfy any concerns. She attended and participated in the planning meetings and raised appropriate questions to ensure all industry requirements and expectations were in accordance with best practices. She kept everyone informed when things took an unexpected turn.

The process was seamless, and everything was accomplished in a timely manner without incident. She gave us some teachable moments and exhibited a calm demeanor when emotions became challenging. Rhonda's work ethics far exceeded our expectations because she left no stone unturned.

Two thumbs up for providing a valuable service. We give our heartfelt thanks to Rhonda for a job well done.

The Norried Family

You Carried My Burden

Dear Rhonda,

Thank you for helping me make Homegoing arrangements for my son, Cpl. Jacai Colson. Your support helped make a difficult time a little more bearable and allowed me and my family to make it through the days leading up to Jacai's services.

Words cannot express the love, kindness, patience and caring support you provided during this difficult time. Because of your support, Jacai's legacy was truly honored during the ceremony. Your wisdom and support were very much appreciated.

I also want to thank you for following up with me in teaching me how to handle an estate. My family is truly blessed to have you guide and continually check on us through this entire process.

Galatians 6:2 "Carry each other's burdens, and in this way, you will fulfill the law of Christ." During this time, you carried my burden and helped me make it through. May God continue to bless and keep you in his grace!!!

Much love and prayer,

Sheila Colson

A Dad with a Plan

It was late summer 2017 when my father got sick suddenly out of nowhere, and it appeared that he wasn't going to recover. Because I'm the youngest, I wanted to panic because I needed my daddy. When it became clear to me that my dad's health wasn't going to get better, unless God stepped in to work a miracle, I called Rhonda Green, who handles funeral services at my church. I didn't know how to prepare final records and papers, and my dad wasn't really open to talking about it. Rhonda told me how important it was to talk about his plan at the right time.

I prayed about it and wanted God to make Daddy open for us to prepare his last will and testament and all his important documents. You see, my dad was a very private, old-school country man. One day, to my surprise, Daddy called me and asked me about getting in touch with "that lady from the church." I called Rhonda, and she came to meet my dad.

When she arrived, Daddy had reservations. I could see it on his face. I marveled at Rhonda's approach to making him feel comfortable and at ease. She never mentioned sickness or death. She respected him by calling him "Dad," and, amazingly, I watched him open up and give her all the information that was needed to ensure his final records were in order.

On March 9, 2018, dad passed away, and everything Rhonda did made our process seamless. I could never repay her or thank her enough for her special gift. I love the anointing that rests on her life for this kind of ministry.

I strongly advise people to do the work NOW, because all of us have a guaranteed date with death, and our loved ones need to be assured our desires are carried out. This is also a great opportunity to alleviate unnecessary drama that shows up when a person transitions.

Thank you, Rhonda, from the bottom of my heart. My family is forever grateful.

Grace and Peace,

Reverend Stephen A. Hurd

UNEXPECTED TRAGEDY WITH NO PLAN IN SIGHT

The day I met Ray, he seemed strong and confident. The quintessential military man. Smart. Alert. At attention. Keenly aware of his surroundings. Not at all the man who laid in a hospital bed clinging to life after quadruple bypass surgery. Everyone, including his nurse, thought he'd recover and eventually return home. He did not. Only God is the author and finisher of life. The period at the end comes from Him. Ray's period at the end came just a few days after his surgery. He died on June 28, 2018.

The day we met, he stood in his Air Force blues with the light of a stained-glass window cascading behind him, at Mt. Calvary Baptist Church, and seemed to me taller than his five-foot-eleven frame. His stance was strong and sure. We were introduced and after some time became friends and eventually husband and wife.

When he died, I knew nothing other than I had to be strong for our adult children and somehow through a myriad of emotions make decisions and arrangements that would honor his life. After meeting with the funeral home, I called my dear friend Dr. Gayle Jones, who immediately spoke with Rhonda. Fortunately, Rhonda found it in her heart to take my hand and walk me through every step in coordinating Ray's service. It was the most elegant and respectful service, and I am much appreciative of Rhonda for her natural skill in guiding me through both before and after service details.

Ray did not have an Exit Plan, so we were left to determine how to best order his memorial service in a way that would honor his life. It was glorious. Rhonda even arranged for the military to attend and perform a flag ceremony and a gun salute, at which I was presented with the flag (and later the bullets from the salute) that now rest safely in a special place in our home. I honestly don't know what I would have done without her!

Because Ray did not have an Exit Plan in place, with Rhonda's help, I was left to navigate through funeral homes, cremation procedures, mounds of paperwork, the Register of Wills, military protocol, the Department of Veterans Affairs, miscellaneous military departments, and the list goes on! After my experience, I have strongly advised my loved ones to put an Exit Plan in place. Grieving families are so captured with loss that having to focus on extreme details of services, gathering important papers, and other necessary activities after a death makes the experience unbearable at times.

I thank God for Rhonda, who stepped into place to ensure my family was cared for and Ray memorialized with the utmost care.

If you don't have an Exit Plan in place, do it now!

C. Janel Powell Kennedy

From the Heart of a Wife

When my husband, Smile Saint Aubin, suddenly passed away, my children and I were devastated. We were in total disbelief that this loving and dedicated husband of 35 years and this awesome father was gone. We adored and cherished our every moment with him, and we honored him as the head of our family. While serving at the White House, he never missed a beat celebrating us and making sure that we had everything that we needed.

The day that Smile passed, we did not know where to start with funeral arrangements. We were introduced to Rhonda Green, and with her knowledge, help, and compassion, we were able to have a wonderful homegoing service for him.

Over the past ten years, we have learned the importance of getting our affairs in order. I have shared the Exit Plan with several of my family members, and I must say, knowing what you are going to do in advance really helps to make the transition a lot smoother.

Rhonda has truly been a blessing to not only our family but the Haitian community as well.

I challenge anyone who is reading this book to complete your Exit Plan and get your house in order, so that your family will not have to make decisions at the last minute.

Our children—Rico, Sandy, and Stephanie—continue to miss their dad. We are grateful that God blessed us with a beautiful granddaughter, Chloe, who reminds us daily of Smile.

With love,

Marie Saint Aubin

WE BELIEVE IN HAVING AN EXIT PLAN

If anyone would have told me in July of 1985 that God was connecting me to a person who would also assist me and my family through the most trying times, I would not have understood the depth of the impending relationship. But after over thirty years of being a part of our family, Rhonda D. Green has been an angel as she shared her gift of helping in crisis.

Years ago, the passion that Rhonda possesses for hurt people became evident, especially in the area of loss of a loved one. Rhonda's main goal is to serve with excellence, seeking God's guidance in what she does. I know from personal experience that Rhonda's calm and loving demeanor is shown regardless of who the loved one is. Our family has lost multiple family members in just a short span of time. The beauty, especially with the last ones, was the fact that pre-planning was done, as we had discussed the Exit Plan across state lines.

Prior to 2015, our immediate family had experienced the sudden transition of two members. My niece, JaQuanda Jones passed in 1999 and my brother-in-law Elder Jonathan Moultrie in 2006. Nothing could prepare us, however, for the loss of my sister Eloise Fairley in 2015, and, only four days later, my sister Pauletta Jones transitioned! They had Exit Plans in place which took some of the stress off of us as a family. Pauletta had her obituary and program written with names of who would do what! That's planning your exit!

It wasn't over. Extended family losses followed, including my mother-in-law in 2016. Then, in 2017, my Father, Bishop C. L. Lorick, Sr., was called home to be with the Lord. My brother, Bishop C. L. Lorick, Jr., followed his hero from earth to reward only sixteen days later. Our attention was on Momma who had lost three children and her husband of seventy years in sixteen months! Rhonda stood by us checking in periodically and assisting over the miles where possible.

Again, having plans in place including insurance and wills proved to be invaluable when everyone was operating on automatic and with overwhelmed hearts.

My family members and I are grateful to God for using Rhonda's knowledge of procedures and agencies to make the end-of-life decisions easier and timely through the Exit Plan. I love my family, so my Exit Plan is ready, which will lessen their pain when I'm gone. Thank you, Rhonda, for being willing to be used by God as He works through you and brings peace of mind through a prepared Exit Plan!

Luv Ya,

Geneva Pearson

Chapter Fourteen

NUGGETS FOR FUNERAL COORDINATORS

Whether you are planning a small memorial service or coordinating a large-scale funeral, you should have the necessary tools, knowledge, and resources to effectively implement a well-coordinated service.

In times of bereavement and sorrow, it is important for the church family to pull together to ensure that proper care, effective planning, and enough resources are available when families need them most.

While death is 100 percent inevitable, only 25 percent of us do any type of end-of-life planning, such as advance medical directives and pre-planned funeral arrangements; shockingly, that leaves 75 percent of us unprepared when there's a death in the family.

As the first in line to receive a call at a time of loss, be prepared and positioned to step up and be a source of guidance, comfort, and spiritual encouragement to families.

HOW TO EFFECTIVELY PLAN AND COORDINATE A FUNERAL OR MEMORIAL

The information below is the general process my funeral services department team uses at FBCG. Some details have been removed to protect FBCG's proprietary information.

The Process

1. Death Notice

   A. Capture the name, relationship, and contact number of the caller.
   B. Send an email to the Funeral and Receptionist Teams with the information.

2. Transfer the caller to the funeral line (answering service).
3. Card Ministry List

   A. The Receptionist Team will place the family on the Card Ministry list. Please be sure to capture the mailing address of the family.

4. Verify Membership

   A. Check the church database to verify the caller's or the decedent's membership.

5. Family Contact

   A. The Funeral Services Team will contact the family (no later than 24 hours from the initial call).

6. Room Request

   A. Check with the Events Scheduling Department to confirm availability of date and space required for service.

7. Communication with the Team

   A. Staff Ministers: Eulogist, Presider, Scripture, and Prayer
   B. Events Department: Room Setup
   C. Music & Arts Department: Musician
   D. BMS: Audio /Video Support
   E. Catering: Repast
   F. Marketing: Website Notification
   G. Church Staff: Email Notification
   H. Deaf or Spanish Ministry if needed

8. Meeting with Family

   A. Personal requests
   B. Viewing policy
   C. Repast (Food & Kitchen) policy
   D. If there is a cost associated with the service, share that information upfront so that the family can make a decision.

Cost of Service Categories

1. Members, minor children, or legal dependent (adult disabled child) of an FBCG member (no charge)
2. Parents, spouse, or adult child over the age of 21 years of an FBCG member
3. Sisters, brothers, or grandparents of an FBCG member
4. Non-member

Donations in Lieu of Flowers

1. FBCG will donate to a non-profit organization of the family's choice in the name of the deceased.

2. We have a donation criterion for the Pastor's office for other pastors and their family members, church leaders, members, and immediate family of members.

Repasts

The church will provide a repast for up to 100 people at no cost for FBCG members, minor child or legal dependent of an FBCG member (adult disabled child). There is a per person charge for additional people and for the following categories below:

1. Parents, spouse, or adult child over the age of 21, of an FBCG member.
2. Sisters, brothers, and grandparents.
3. Non-members with no association with FBCG.

Program Preparation, Design, and Printing

Family completing program or FBCG completing program:

1. If FBCG completes the program for the family, we will need the obituary, names of people giving remarks, pall bearers, photos, poems, and any special messages to be included in the program. Depending on the type of program that the family desires, there may be a fee.

2. If family completes the program, we will provide the family with a copy of our standard order of service to include in the program.

Requests for the Pastor to Eulogize

The family may request the pastor or a specific staff minister to eulogize.

A. Advise the family that you will forward their request to the Pastoral Office or to the Ministerial Team Leader.
B. Do not make any promises until you are sure who will be assigned to the service.

Volunteer and Staff Support

Request support and assistance from the volunteers and team to carry out the service (e.g., folding programs, checking with ushers to see if more programs are needed, directing guest clergy, ensuring program participants are in place, etc.).

High-Profile Services

1. Police and Fire Departments
   A. Know the difference in requirements for a person killed in the line of duty versus natural causes.
   B. Work with county officials for seating, parking, etc.
2. Politicians and Government Officials
3. Church Leaders
4. Police Escort to Cemetery

Member Care

The death of a loved one often opens a floodgate of emotions. When planning a funeral or memorial service to honor, remember, and celebrate the lives of loved ones, we walk alongside families during their season of grief. The FBCG Funeral Services Team assists by providing support, comfort, and help while designing a meaningful funeral or memorial service.

1. How to provide end-to-end care for leaders and members of your church:

   A. Prior to illness
   B. After death

2. Direct family to your local Register of Wills Office.
3. Assist family with contact information for the Veterans Administration, Office of Personnel Management, and Social Security Office.
4. Work with families to diffuse conflicts in order to finalize funeral arrangements.

Services Held for Members at Other Locations

If the deceased is an FBCG member and the service will not be held at FBCG, please follow the related steps above under "The Process."

Community Services

1. If the deceased is not an FBCG member or an immediate family member of an FBCG member, this will be reviewed on a case-by-case basis and subject to availability.

2. If another church requests to use our sanctuary for a funeral service, please adhere to the following:

   A. Inform the person who is calling that the pastor of the requesting church must call the Senior Pastor's office for authorization.
   B. Notify the Senior Pastor's office to expect a call for use of the sanctuary.
   C. If the request is approved, share our policies and procedures with the contact person, and be available to assist on the day of the service.

SELF CARE

I Became Overwhelmed

I recall waking up one morning full of tears. I couldn't figure out what was wrong with me. I cried for several hours until it hit me that I had to get ready for work. I had two services to coordinate that day.

The first service was for a person that I was very close to. As I entered the sanctuary, my heart fluttered, and my eyes filled with tears again. It was at that moment I realized that I was grieving. I did all I could to get myself together so I could get the service started and make it through the day.

I knew I was in over my head when I could not stay seated during the funeral. After three trips to the restroom and half a box of tissues, I shared with one of my leaders that I was overwhelmed with funerals. She prayed with me and assured me that help was on the way. My heaviness caused her to wonder if anyone else who served funerals might also be overwhelmed. Little did I know, there were several others.

My employer contacted a resource, and everyone that worked funerals at my church attended an informative session. This session proved to be rewarding. It helped me to deal with my emotions. Being able to process through how I felt is what saved me. However, I realized that we all need to continue with our mental health care in order to be healthy and stable.

How to Avoid Burnout

Whether we are serving on our job, in our family or for a close friend, death can bring about several emotions for anyone working funerals. After coordinating numerous funerals over the years, I realized that I had to slow down and take time to grieve the loved ones that transitioned in my life.

Having a person who specializes in grief therapy was a great help to me. Here are a few tips that have helped me over the years to avoid burnout:

Planning

- I take time to plan every service as close to receiving the death notification as possible. This way, I avoid having to arrange several funerals at one time, which can be very stressful.
- I then confirm the date and availability of the required support staff.

Knowledge

- We should know the circumstances of the death. Having support staff informed and ready to assist allows us to keep our focus on our assignments.
- Whether it's the Bereavement Team for a homicide case, the Spiritual Cares Team for the death of an infant or the Cancer Support Team for one who has lost their battle with illness, their support will allow us to serve the next family with ease and peace of mind.

Resting, Eating and Taking Prescribed Medications

- We should get proper rest so that we will be alert and ready to serve. If we are serving while exhausted, it is not good for our health or our mental state.
- Taking time to eat proper meals will help us mentally and physically. Missing meals can cause us to be weak and lethargic.
- When we are under a doctor's care and taking prescribed medication, we need to follow the instructions given to us. I keep a supply of my medicine in my office just in case I forget to take it before leaving home.

Support

- We should know when to push back and get help. It is helpful to talk to team members and grief counselors.

- Use the resources that are offered by your employer. On my job, our Spiritual Cares Department provides biblically-based, clinically-informed counseling services to help with soul care and spiritual direction needs pertaining to areas of grief and loss, emotional and spiritual concerns. We also have access to an Employee Assistance Program (EPA) who offers confidential and professional counseling. The help is there, we just have to use it.

- Have a debriefing meeting to diffuse the emotions following homicides, suicides, multiple deaths, and other high-profile services that may cause stress.

- Funeral directors and coordinators spend a great amount of time taking care of other people. Taking care of one's self should be one of the primary requirements for working in this field.

- I am sure there are organizations for licensed funeral directors who offer educational resources, but after searching the web, I was not able to find a suitable group for unlicensed funeral staff.

- Before teaching a workshop on "Planning and Coordinating Funerals that Give Hope and Comfort" at our 2019 Beyond Conference, I decided to look into starting a small support group for those of us who coordinate funerals and would like to have a network to share ideas with or to gain support. If you are an unlicensed funeral coordinator or a bereavement team member and are interested in being a part of this group, please send me an email at myexitplan@rhondadgreen.org.

GRIEF AND BEREAVEMENT

DEALING WITH GRIEF

Dealing with grief can be overwhelming for most people. In some cases, a person may realize that they are not coping at a normal level and will reach out for help. Others may have a difficult time figuring out what is going on with them. If help is needed, it is very important to get help!

Death can come unexpectedly with adults and children. Sudden accidents or tragedies can increase the intensity of grief. I believe that having your affairs in order for children as well as adults can decrease the stress of trying to figure out how to pay for the services, and it can help you to move along swiftly versus having to wait until funds are collected to carry out your wishes.

When an adult dies without a plan in place, it's a recipe for extreme hardship on a family. I am working with a mother today who is having a difficult time moving forward because of her grief. She is unable to return to work and has multiple episodes a week of crying and not being able to cope with everyday life. Often, she wonders what she could have done prior to the death that would have made a difference. The answer is nothing. We can encourage our family members to make decisions or we can assume that they have already put a plan in place. At the end of the day, when everything is up in the air and nothing is in place, it leaves our lives upside down.

We now must complete the business of her deceased loved one and then get her into counseling and/or a support group. I trust that once she is with others who have experienced an unexpected death, she may be able to identify with someone that feels the same way she does, and together they can support one another.

I become concerned when people have a hard time letting go. Somewhere in my travels, I read an article that said, "We are born to die." My takeaway on that was that every person who is born will someday die. Therefore, I encourage everyone to gather life's memories with your loved ones each day that you are here on earth, and when it's your time to die, you will leave a legacy of memories ... some good and maybe some bad. You should not find yourself stuck in yesteryear and at the cemetery every day talking to your loved one who is not there. Life is for living, and if it was your time to die, you would not be here now reading this book. So, grieve for a while if you must, and then live your life to the fullest each day.

Thirty-five years ago when my first husband passed away, I found myself a single parent of three small children, with the youngest being a disabled child. *How in the world am I going to get through this?* I wondered. Well, God connected me with my childhood sweetheart, whom I later married. Not knowing that I had not processed through my grief, I found myself needing counseling. It was the counseling that helped me to get my life back on track. And today, I celebrate over thirty years of marriage.

In some cases, it's difficult for former in-laws to accept the fact that a person once married to one of their relatives is now getting married to someone else. Once again, *you* did not die! Life goes on, so live it to the fullest. If God sends you a new spouse, go for it! God knows what you need. And if He decides that you will be single for the rest of your life, get together with other singles in your age range and enjoy life. Travel or do whatever it is that you like to do, but just do you!

I must add that one should not make any type of major decisions or commitments immediately after the death of a loved one. This is a very emotional time, and you don't want to make decisions that you will later regret.

GRIEF SUPPORT

There are grief support groups at various organizations and churches. My church offers individual as well as group support for adults and children. You do not have to travel this road alone. If you are having difficulty processing the death of a loved one, when you know you need help, get it!

I met a lady in 1991 while I was working at the Suicide Prevention Center. Her brother had recently committed suicide, and her grandmother, who was like a mom to her, died six weeks prior to her brother. Ten years later her dad died. The lady joined one of my support groups because she was having a rough time dealing with her grief.

She worked in Washington, DC, at the time, moved back to her hometown in Philadelphia to help with her niece and nephew who had lost their father and six months later lost their mother to a heart attack. About two years later, she moved to Los Angeles. We continued to stay in contact over the years. Her mom lives on the East Coast and was diagnosed with dementia after a stroke a few years ago. The lady lost her job shortly after and recently lost all of her retiree benefits. While her mom has a family caregiver living with her, this lady continues to handle her mom's business matters and her care from California. Recognizing that her network of family and friends is very small, I shared the tools of *My Exit Plan* with her. She was always worried about what would happen to her should she become ill and/or die in LA. I encouraged her to get her affairs in order.

Here it is twenty-eight years later, and she still has not recovered from her grief. I share this story because everyone's situation is not the same. Some people can process their grief and move forward, and for others it takes longer.

Another client was having such a hard time dealing with the death of her son that I felt compelled to do something to help her. She was not ready for a support group, but something needed to happen. As I prayed for her, I started thinking about how I moved through my grief when my mom died. Helping other people had taken the focus off me, and before I knew it, I was sharing my grief story and telling others that they too can be healed. I then realized that my client likewise needed to share her story so that other mothers would not have to experience what she did. I asked her to give her testimony at an Exit Plan symposium so that other sons and daughters would understand why it is so important to have their affairs in order, not leaving their parents with a temporary financial hardship and so much to do.

Well, my dear client was not feeling this speaking thing, but I encouraged her to go through with it. I believed that, as with me, this would help her move through her grief and identify with her feelings of guilt and anger. She would come to understand that she was a loving mother and had done everything that she could for her son. She would also understand that there was nothing else she could have done beyond encouraging him to get a will or trust and make sure his affairs were in order. Once she comes to grip with this reality, she will be on the road to healing and a ministry of helping others. After sharing this with her, she began to see herself walking in this light. She spoke at the event, and it was amazing how she captured the attention of the audience when she spoke about her son. She did an awesome job!

KNOWING WHAT TO SAY AND WHAT NOT TO SAY

Some people don't know what to say to a grieving person. If you find yourself in that position, sometimes it's best to just give a smile, hug, or handshake and keep moving. When a person has experienced death, the last thing they need is someone telling them how they should feel. And if you ask a person who has just lost their spouse, "How do you feel?" what do you really expect them to say? On the other hand, when they are at peace and say that they are fine, you can't respond with, "No, you are not."

I know that most people mean well and want to support the people around them, but please think before you speak. Does what you are about to say make sense? Is it going to make the person angry? Will it make them sad? Just asking them how they are doing is probably the wrong question from the beginning. You know they just had a death in their family, so how do you expect them to be? Maybe just saying "Praying for you, my friend," or something along those lines will help. Keep it simple, yet warm and endearing. Telling people to call you if they need anything ... do you really mean that? Will you go to their need if they call?

I sat with a friend once who returned to work after a death in his family, and we laughed about the things people say when they don't know what to say. I was honored to be able to share that laugh with a person who was grieving and encourage them to hang it there. In a few weeks, things will get back to a new normal for him.

The following resources are available to assist you:

1. Government agencies that may be needed when a death occurs. This list includes contact numbers for Social Security, Office of Personnel Management, and Veterans Affairs.

2. Information on Grief Support Groups for children and adults.

3. Books that are available in bookstores and online on grief and bereavement.

4. The Exit Plan Workbook, a resource I created that is designed to walk you step-by-step in gathering essential information so that your loved ones can fulfill your wishes as they celebrate your life in death.

5. Definitions for estate matters.

Government Agencies

Office of Personnel Management: 1-888-767-6738
www.opm.gov

Social Security Administration: 1-800-772-1213
www.ssa.gov

Veterans Affairs: 1-800-827-1000
www.va.gov

Grief Support Groups

Grief Share
www.griefshare.org/

Grief Support
www.griefsupport.com/

The Healing Transitions and Bereavement Ministry of First Baptist Church of Glenarden

The Healing Ministry Transistion and Bereavement Ministry offers a ministry of support for those who are suffering the loss of a loved one.

For more information, email_htb@fbcglenarden.org

Books on Grief and Bereavement

The Grief Recovery Handbooks - ISBN #: 9780061686078

Grieving God's Way - ISBN #: 9780849947223

Grieving the Loss of a Loved One - ISBN #: 9780310358725

Grieving the Loss of Someone You Love - ISBN #: 9780800725501

Grief: Living At Peace with Loss - ISBN #: 9781596366572

Estate Definitions[5]

Administration of an estate: the management of a decedent's assets, which includes the collection of property, payment of expenses and debts, and distribution to the heirs or legatees.

Administrative Probate: a proceeding that is initiated by an interested person with the Register of Wills for the appointment of a personal representative and for the probate of a will, or the determination of intestacy of the decedent.

Child (or children): a child who is a legitimate child, an adopted child, an illegitimate child to the extent provided by law, and a child conceived from the genetic material of a person after the death of the person to the extent provided by law.

Claimant: a person (or entity) who files a claim against a decedent's estate.

Debt of record: a recorded debt, such as a mortgage on real property, that is recorded in land records.

Decedent: a deceased person.

Descendant: one who is in the bloodline of an ancestor. (Descendants include child, grandchild, great-grandchild, etc.)

Domicile: the place where a person has physically been present with the intention to make the place a permanent home. (In other words, domicile is the place one would return to or intend to return to when away.)

Election against the will: the right provided by statute to a spouse that allows him/her to receive a statutory share, even if it is more than the will provided.

Encumbrance: a lien or claim attached to property, such as a mortgage on real property.

Estate: the property of a decedent.

Family allowance: an allowance in addition to property passing under the will or by the laws of intestacy, for the personal use of the surviving spouse and for the use of each unmarried child under the age of eighteen years.

Fiduciary: a person or institution that manages and administers money and

---

5 Information from the Prince George's County Register of Wills website, http://registers.maryland.gov/main/princegeorges.html.

other assets of another. A fiduciary includes trustee, receiver, custodian, guardian, executor, administrator, or personal representative.

Gross estate: the actual value of the estate assets without the deduction of liens, debts, or expenses.

Heir: a family member who inherits from an estate under the laws of intestacy (from a decedent who died without a will).

Information Report: the document that reports all non-probate property (property that passes outside the probate estate). (Non-Probate property includes, but is not limited to, jointly held assets, life estate or remainder interests in a trust or deed, trusts in which the decedent had an interest, payable on death (P.O.D.) assets, and pension and benefit plans including IRAs with named beneficiaries.)

Inheritance tax: a tax imposed on the privilege of receiving property from a decedent's estate.

Interested person: the person(s) serving (or petitioning to serve) as personal representative(s), legatees, heirs (even if the decedent died testate), trustee(s) of a testamentary trust, trustee(s) of a living trust, if applicable, and court-appointed guardian(s) for minors and disabled adults who are interested persons.

Intestate: without a will.

Issue: every living lineal descendant except a lineal descendant of a living lineal descendant, including a legitimate child, an adopted child, an illegitimate child to the extent provided by law, and a child conceived from the genetic material of a person after the death of the person to the extent provided by law. Issue does not include a stepchild or a foster child.

Joint tenancy: a type of ownership where personal or real property is held jointly by two or more persons in undivided (equal) shares with the right of survivorship. When a joint tenant dies, his/her share passes automatically by operation of law to the survivor(s).

Judicial probate: a probate proceeding conducted by the Orphans' Court (as opposed to the Register of Wills) when the situation prohibits administrative probate (such as, validity of the will is questioned, will is damaged, or more than one qualified person applies for personal representative).

Legatee: a person named in a will to receive.

Letter of Administration: a document issued by the Register of Wills that authorizes a personal representative to administer an estate.

Limited Order: an order allowing for the search of assets in the decedent's name alone or the will located in a safe deposit box in the name of the decedent.

Lineal: heir or legatee: one who is of the direct line of the decedent.

Modified Administration: a streamlined version of administrative probate available to the personal representative (in estates where the decedent died on or after October 1, 1997). In lieu of an inventory and an account, the personal representative is required to file a final report within 10 months from the date of appointment. (See Section 8 of this booklet for details.)

Net estate: property remaining after the deduction of liens, debts, and expenses.

Non-probate estate: property that passes outside the probate estate, includes, but not limited to jointly held assets, life estate or remainder interests in a trust **or deed,** trusts in which the decedent had an interest, payable on death (P.O.D.) assets, and pension and benefit plans including IRAs with named beneficiaries.

Personal Representative: the person appointed to administer the estate (often referred to as executor or administrator).

Petition for Probate: the document required to initiate a probate proceeding.

Pour-over Will: a will giving money or property to an existing trust.

Probate estate: property owned solely by the decedent or as a tenant in common.

Regular estate: the estate procedure for a decedent who owned probate assets with a gross value in excess of $50,000 (or $100,000 if the sole heir or legatee is the surviving spouse).*

Residence: living in a specific area without necessarily having the intent to indefinitely stay there (See Domicile for the difference.).

Small estate: the estate procedure for a decedent who owned probate assets with a gross value of $50,000 or less (or $100,000 or less if the sole heir or legatee is the surviving spouse).*

Special Administrator: an administrator of an estate appointed by the court when it is necessary to protect and manage property prior to the appointment of a personal representative. (A special administrator has limited powers.)

Tenants by the entirety: a type of ownership that is created only between husband and wife where they hold title to an interest in property together, with the right of survivorship upon the death of the first to die.

Tenants in common: a type of ownership where two or more persons each hold an undivided interest in a piece of property with no right of survivorship. Upon the death of an owner, his/her interest passes to the heirs under the laws of intestacy, or in accordance with the terms of the will.

Testamentary Trust: a trust that is created by a will and takes effect when the settlor (testator/ testatrix) dies.

Testate: dying with a will.

Testator/testatrix: male/female who makes a will.

Trust, also living trust or inter vivos trust: real and/or personal property held by one party (trustee) for the benefit of another (beneficiary). Trust assets are non-probate assets.

To purchase the *My Exit Plan Workbook*
or to obtain more information, visit the website:
www.myexitplan-mep.com

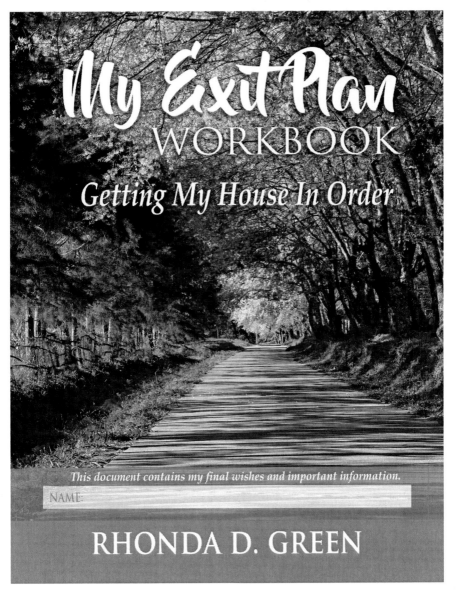

Have a question? Email Us:
myexitplan@rhondagreen.org

FROM THE AUTHOR

We generally look forward to preparing for major life events such as a birth, wedding, or retirement. However, how many of us prepare for our final farewell? Many of us either don't want to think about death right now or would rather wait until that time comes. There's a passage in II Kings 20:1 when Hezekiah was near death. Isaiah the prophet went to him and said, "Thus says the LORD: 'Set your house in order, for you shall die and not live.'" This is a lesson for us all because King Solomon, the wisest man who ever lived, instructs us that death is inevitable (Ecclesiastes 3:1–2).

This book is not just for you but also for your loved ones. I am excited that today people are not only calling me to their bedside to "get their house in order" when they are told that their illness is terminal, they are also catching on to completing their Exit Plan and having their affairs in order in advance. *Remember, you can't take it with you!*

The key to it all is that once you "get your house in order," you don't have to talk about death anymore … you can focus on living until God calls you home.

"Having an Exit Plan provides clarity and comfort to family members and ensures your wishes are honored."